D1586049

MORT GALE
who revealed the secrets of
Biorhythm Compatibility
invites you to explore the potential of
MOON POWER

"I have developed simple tables for finding the moon's phases and signs for any date. It will take you less than 30 seconds to do it. I show you how to compare the moon's position in your life with its position in another person's life, to estimate the likelihood of a compatible relationship between the two of you. You will see the link between the moon and menstruation and learn why female reproductive functions follow the phases of the moon. I will tell you about new ways being used to regain menstrual regularity by imitating the light of a Full Moon. And about how others use the positions of the moon for selecting the sex of their next child."

Begin now to gain a better understanding of how the moon affects your life.

Begin now to use MOON POWER.

Also by Mort Gale

Biorhythm Compatibility

Published by
WARNER BOOKS

MOON POWER

BY
MORT GALE

WARNER BOOKS

A Warner Communications Company

Warner Books are
distributed in the
United Kingdom by

HAMLYN PAPERBACKS

WARNER BOOKS EDITION

Copyright © 1980 by Mort Gale
All rights reserved.

ISBN: 0-446-82988-9

Cover art by Janice Miamoto

Warner Books, Inc., 75 Rockefeller Plaza, New York, N.Y. 10019

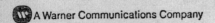 A Warner Communications Company

Printed in the United States of America

First Printing: February, 1980

10 9 8 7 6 5 4 3 2

To my parents,
Abraham and Sarah,

For teaching me the love of learning,
and the joy of sharing it with others

Contents

Tables

Figures

MOON POWER

Preface

The moon affects the way you feel. Not just when there is a Full Moon. But all the time. Sometimes the moon can make you feel warm and sexy. Other times it can turn you cool, or turn you off. Or make you angry. Or depressed. It can even set you up for a stupid illness, or a nasty accident. It all depends on where the moon is in the sky, compared to where it was on the day you were born.

There's nothing new in this belief. People have believed in moon power for centuries. Not only the astrologers. Farmers noticed how the moon influenced their crops, so they planted by the moon to get a better yield. Others noticed how the changing phases of the moon brought on changes in the behavior of people. But we still haven't learned how to use the moon to understand other people, or even ourselves. Partly because people are more complicated than crops. But mostly because the ancient moon beliefs are still regarded as "silly superstitions."

Fortunately, this is changing. Scientists are now looking into old moon beliefs and finding that many of them are perfectly valid. They are bringing new tools to the task of detecting the moon's effects on life. And, you ask yourself, what's the moon doing to *my* life?

This book shows you! It starts with the basics. First, it tells you something about how the moon moves around the earth. Then you will see how that motion is described in terms of the moon's phases and the moon signs, or positions in the zodiac. And how these phases and signs tell you the status of your changing environment. You will see that, as your lunar environment changes, it affects your body chemistry. This depends on how your present lunar environment compares with that into which you were born. You will learn how to compare these environments by comparing the position of the moon on any date with its position on the date you were born. When you do that, you can find out which lunar environments make you feel great, and which cause you trouble. You can then anticipate those days by recognizing which moon phases and signs bring you those environments.

This may be starting to sound complicated and difficult. I assure you that it's not. You don't have to know anything about astronomy or science to be able to check out the moon's influence on your life. All you need is the desire to do so. I'll take you from there.

I have developed simple tables for finding the moon's phases and signs for any date. It will take you less than thirty seconds to do it. I have also developed a simple way for you to examine these phases and signs to help you spot the moon's influence in your life. I even show you how to compare the moon's position in your life with its position in another person's life, to estimate the likelihood of a compatible relationship between the two of you.

Many of you will be especially interested in the chapter dealing with the influence of the moon on women. You will see the link between the moon and menstruation, and learn why female reproductive functions follow the phases of the moon. I will tell you about new ways being used to regain menstrual regularity by imitating the light of a Full Moon. And how others use the positions of the moon for selecting the sex of their child.

18

Others of you may be more curious about how the moon affects you astrologically. If you are like most people, you know your sun sign, and the signs of a few close friends. You probably also have a general idea about the characteristics attributed to those signs. But you probably don't know your moon sign, or the moon's phase on the day you were born. Or what they might mean.

You can easily find these signs and phases from the simple tables in Chapter 4. Then you can go to Chapter 8 to find out what the astrologers have to say about how your moon sign modifies your character and behavior patterns.

I hope that this book may stimulate some of you into doing your own research into the influences of the moon. The variety of tables and charts I have developed should help you do that with a minimum of effort. You may, for instance, want to see what the moon has to do with your bad moods, your best relationships, or the probable sex of your unborn child. You may want to look at lunar effects on the stock market. There are many unsuspected facets of life that probably reflect the influence of the moon. And they will remain hidden until enough people, perhaps some of you, have the courage to look into "silly superstitions" in search of the nuggets of truth that lie hidden under the myths about "moon power."

You will notice that I have not written this book in the academic tradition of quoting sources in the text or in footnotes. I felt that such a treatment might be distracting to many readers. Instead, I have provided references at the end of the book for those who care to dig more deeply into this fascinating subject. Many of these references have extensive bibliographies which in turn can lead you to other sources for as far as you care to go.

I would like to express my thanks to those who have been especially helpful to me as I wrote this book. Only an author's wife can know what her husband means when he says, in an acknowledgment, "Thank you." Thank you, Maureen, for your faith and your patience. And again, for loving me.

Many of the insights which led to the material in this book were based on personal information which was generously provided by family and friends. I would like them each to know how grateful I am for their help and trust. Thank you, Alayne Gale and Debbie Connell, Susan Garson and Debbie Giffen, Rochelle Kraft, Judith Dimmerman, Harriet Miller, Yvonne Panitch, Cookie and Michele Mattioli, and Frannie Uff. Your secrets are safe with me. But the insights they gave me I share with the world.

A special thanks to Kathleen Malley, for her continued confidence, encouragement and support.

1
Moon Beliefs

Introduction

People have been looking up at the moon for millions of years. Actually, its hard to ignore the moon. It's the biggest thing that you can see in the sky. And then, as if to attract your attention, it keeps changing its shape every day. These changing shapes, or *phases*, go through a complete cycle once a month. At first you can't see the moon at all. That's called the New Moon, since it begins the cycle. Then you see it as a thin crescent which grows into a half moon in about a week. It continues to grow until it becomes a Full Moon by the end of the second week. Then, the order is reversed, and the moon becomes a half moon by the end of the third week. It shrinks to a crescent, and finally into total darkness again by the end of the fourth week.

It's easy to see how these regular changes in the moon's shape became the basis for the earliest calendars. The time between Full Moons is about thirty days. That means that there are about twelve Full Moons each year, three for each of the seasons. Anyone who watched the moon would soon notice how its changing phases correlated with the seasonal activities on earth. Two moons from planting a crop to its harvest. Nine moons for a pregnancy, and so on.

It's a small step from counting Full Moons to noticing what happens between one Full Moon and the next. Certain crops planted under the light of a Full Moon will grow better than if they were planted under the dark of the moon. Other crops seem to be favored if they are started under a New Moon. The folklore of every people is rich in its advice about what is to be done and what is to be avoided under the different phases of the moon. It is surprising how similar these moon beliefs are in the folklore of different cultures, from all parts of the world.

However, these beliefs in the moon's powers were based on more than just the observations of its monthly phases. Other, more careful, observers had noticed changes in the elevation of the moon as it passed across the skies each night. Sometimes the moon would pass low across the sky. Then, two weeks later, it would be much higher as it crossed the sky. These changing altitudes also followed a monthly cycle, but one different from the cycle of moon phases.

As the moon crossed the sky at these heights, people saw it against a different background of distant stars. These star groups, known as the signs of the zodiac, were used to mark the altitude of the moon on any date. That was important—the height of the moon, they saw, influenced the outcome of many activities. So the moon-watchers then remembered these heights in terms of the moon's sign in the zodiac.

Tides and the Weather

Perhaps the best way to show how various beliefs about the moon come into existence is to show how easy it is to discover one for yourself. All it takes is some patience, and an interest in careful observation. Let's say that you decided to take your vacation at a seaside resort. Each morning, before breakfast, you go down to watch the waves roar up onto the beach. As you sit there on the sand, you notice that each of the waves climbs higher as it washes up toward your feet. And

22

then, after a pause, they begin to recede with each successive wave. You have just seen the passing of a high tide. As you lie back on the sand you happen to notice the moon overhead. You even recognize it as a Last Quarter Moon, with its curved side facing to your left. You look at your watch. It's seven o'clock, time to go in for breakfast.

The next day you oversleep but decide to go down to watch the waves anyway. And again you see the advancing waves, followed by a retreat of the successive waves. As you look up into another clear sky you see the moon just where you saw it the day before. But now, as you look at your watch, it is 7:50 A.M., still time for breakfast.

If you decided to keep track of these observations, you would jot down the times of these high tides along with the position and shape of the moon. After collecting your observations you would discover the following pattern. You would notice that the highest waves arrive fifty minutes later each day, and that the moon was always overhead at that time. Furthermore, you would see that the highest tides occurred under a Full Moon and again under a New Moon, and always at midnight and noon.

If no one had yet noticed this connection between high tides and the moon's passage overhead, and if you had the courage to do so, you could claim the discovery that the moon causes high tides. You would have started a moon belief. Any moon belief begins with a set of careful observations, plus the insight to see a connection between them. And the courage to announce it to the world for its approval or its ridicule.

In the case of the moon and the tides, though, somebody got there before you did. The first person who is credited with claiming that the moon influenced the tides was a Greek, Poseidonius of Apamea. That was in 100 B.C. For over a thousand years his moon belief was accepted by some and denounced by others as a superstition. That's because no one could offer an understandable explanation for *how* the moon influenced the tides. Reason, based on the knowledge of the times, argued that the tiny moon in the distant heavens couldn't pos-

23

sibly have the power to lift the massive oceans in daily tides. And so, it remained a matter of moon belief versus logic and reason for about seventeen hundred years.

Nor were those who believed in the moon's power able to defend their belief against its own inconsistencies. If the moon pulled up the tides when it was overhead, then why were there high tides again, about twelve hours later, when the moon was nowhere in sight? The beliefs in the moon's powers were based on one set of observations. And yet these observations were contradicted by another set of observations on the same tides. Which were you to believe? This is still the central problem in searching for the truth behind the moon beliefs that have come down to us through folklore and superstition.

The truth behind the moon belief in the tides was finally resolved in the late seventeenth century. That's when Isaac Newton discovered the law of universal gravitation. He then applied that law to the problem of the tides and found that, indeed, the moon's gravitational forces influence the tides on the earth. He was also able to explain why the tides rise twice a day, twelve hours apart. You'll see why too, when we get to Chapter 3.

Most of the moon beliefs that have come down to us over the centuries are still waiting for other Isaac Newtons to discover their central truths. Happily, some new Newtons are cautiously stepping forward with fresher observations in support of older beliefs—and with newer knowledge. Consider, for example, the effect of the moon on the weather.

Centuries of observations have led to the belief that the moon has an influence on the amount of rainfall, either because of the moon's phase or its position in the zodiac. For a long time, though, meteorologists haven't wanted to test these relationships—they know of no reason for them to be valid, and the observations come to us by way of folklore and superstition. This reluctance to look further is reinforced by ridicule. Consider the following typical debunking: "Equally widespread is the belief that the weather changes with the phases of the moon. It is reduced to absurdity by the simple fact that

24

the changes in the weather varies . . . from place to place . . . while changes in the phases of the moon are seen to change simultaneously all over the earth. In spite of this, the crude superstition is ineradicable, because people remember every change in the weather coinciding with a change in the phase of the moon, while they forget the countless instances where the weather changes without any correlation with the lunar phases." [Robert Eisler, p. 67, *Moon Lore* (T. Harley, Detroit, Singing Tree Press, 1969).]

Thus logic and reason combine to keep you from looking any further into that moon belief But sometimes the evidence is too overwhelming to ignore. Two Australian scientists, E. E. Adderly and E. G. Bowen, examining decades of weather reports, found that the amount of rainfall was clearly connected with the phases of the moon. It rained more often right after a Full Moon and a New Moon than at other times of the month. It was later found that more storms occurred at those times as well.

Yet, when they found this support of an old moon belief they decided not to publish their results: "The reason for doing so was that our work on singularities in rainfall was still being treated with disbelief in meteorological circles, and to suggest a lunar effect on rainfall would simply not have met with the right response." However, when they learned that three Americans had come up with the same results, they all decided to publish their results at the same time. That was in 1962. Another moon belief has moved from the ranks of superstition and entered the realm of scientific fact. And, along with it have come new insights into how the moon may be exercising its powers. In this case, the scientists suggest, the moon may be changing weather by deflecting meteoric dust into our atmosphere and affecting the fields and forces that transfer energies from its upper to its lower regions.

This example is doubly useful—first, it shows how ridicule can delay or prevent the investigation of important matters that happen to the subject of "unfounded" beliefs. Neither of these groups of scientists would have published their findings if they hadn't happened to learn about the other. And we still might not know that the moon does affect the weather.

Second, it shows that a moon belief can be true in a statistical sense as well as in an absolute sense. It depends on how many factors affect the thing that you are observing. The tides are affected primarily by the moon, with lesser effects by the sun. Therefore, a "simple law" can show you the relationship between the moon and the tides. In the case of the weather, the moon is one of many factors that affect the rainfall. Therefore the moon's influence cannot be predicted with any precision. However, its influence will show up in a statistical analysis of the observations. Such an analysis will tell you, on the average, what effects will be more likely to occur under what phases of the moon.

Statistical analyses are beginning to show how the moon's changing positions in the sky can affect our physical environment which in turn affects the biological energies of living things on our earth. Let's take a look at how the moon beliefs tell us what to expect of the moon's power over life and death.

Down on the Farm

Farmers have scheduled their lives according to the moon phases and moon signs for centuries. Their ancient moon beliefs were gradually crystallized into traditions which guided the times for planting and sowing and for doing the daily chores that fill a farmer's life. These were finally written down in almanacs in the form of instructions and timetables for doing everything that had to be done. The almanacs were used to find out when the moon would be in its different phases and signs throughout the year.

If you have the chance, you should look at one of these almanacs. You will be surprised to see how completely the moon's influence was accepted in daily life. As you read, you should keep in mind that many of these beliefs were based on years of observation. Some of these beliefs have been checked by scientific methods and found to be statistically true. Others were checked, with inconclusive results. Careful studies must yet be made before an impartial jury can decide on the truth behind these agricultural moon practices.

Here is a sample of some that guide a farmer's life: Not all crops are to be planted during the same phases of the moon. Plants which have their edible parts above the ground, such as lettuce and corn, should be planted as the light of the moon waxes brighter (that would be during the two weeks between a New Moon and a Full Moon). Crops that grow with their edible parts in the ground, such as beets and potatoes, should be planted as the moon's light is waning (that would be during the two weeks from a Full Moon to a New Moon). Certain plants, such as cabbage, do best if they are planted during the Full Moon. Peas, however, should be planted under a New Moon.

These instructions also include rules for when to plant according to the moon's height, as shown by its sign in the zodiac. Beets, carrots, and radishes do best if they are planted when the moon is in the sign of Pisces. Corn will grow better if it is planted when the moon is in Scorpio. Beans and lentils will do well if planted when the moon is in Cancer, and especially well if that coincides with a Full Moon. But cabbage, which also does well under a Full Moon, will do better if it is planted when a Full Moon happens to be in Aries at the same time. Since the moon will move from one sign of the zodiac to the next in a matter of two or three days, you can see why an almanac was needed to help schedule the work.

Almanacs will provide planting schedules for specific crops, based on these moon beliefs. The schedules are calculated to show when the moon will be in the proper phase and sign best suited for each crop. However, they are then adjusted to account for the various climatic conditions in different parts of the country.

Here are some of the other chores that are scheduled by the moon: Butchering is best done under a waxing moon; that assures fatter and juicier meat. If, instead, hogs are butchered under a waning moon, the meat will swell in the pork barrel. Trees should be cut down for timber near the end of a waning moon. If they are cut

27

during a waxing moon the sap will be up in the wood and it will attract destructive bugs. You should cut your weeds under a waning moon to keep them from growing back too soon. Better still, cut the weeds when the moon is in Gemini, Leo and Virgo.

Even personal matters follow the moon: Cut your hair during a waxing moon if you want it to grow faster. If you want to thin your hair, cut it during a waning moon. The same goes for your nails or corns. Cut them under a waning moon to keep them from growing fast. The best time to get married is under a waxing moon (which is also the best time to move).

These are just a few of the many moon beliefs which have come down to us over the years. They are the ones that focus on the moon's ability to affect the growth of things. However, other moon beliefs, which center around the moon's ability to influence people's behavior and well-being, would be of more immediate interest to those of you who are not farmers. Especially if you are someone who has to deal with many people each day. Let's see what some of these beliefs have to tell us about what to expect of people.

Life in the City

Those of you who live in the cities, surrounded by people, are in the best position to discover the statistical truths behind some of the old moon beliefs. For example, almost everyone knows the theory that the Full Moon brings out all the "crazies." People hit each other more often, and harder, during a Full Moon. They commit more crimes and start more fires. You can check this for yourself, in an unscientific way. All you have to do is keep your eyes open.

You can begin by noticing if there is an increase in the levels of violence at the approach of a Full Moon. One way would be to keep track of the behavior of your friends to see if they become more aggressive during certain phases of the moon. Or, to keep it on an impersonal basis, you can just keep a count of the number of police and fire sirens you hear each night. In either

28

case, you should be able to see an increase in the level of violence during the Full Moon.

You could discover the same thing by talking to those who have to deal with violence. Call up the city desk of a newspaper, the desk sergeants at the police or fire station, or the admissions clerk at the emergency room of a hospital. Ask them if they believe that the Full Moon has an effect on the level of violence that they deal with. Most of them will tell you that it does!

Even though this is an unscientific way to check out an old moon belief, you will find that your results will be the same as those found by more scientific studies. Crime statistics show that the number of rapes, robberies, assaults, child beatings, drunkenness, etc., will all rise on the day of a Full Moon. Other statistics show that more people are admitted to mental hospitals during a Full Moon, and that the inmates who are already there suffer more disturbances at the Full Moon. It seems that the Full Moon does something to your body chemistry that can push you over a threshold into patterns of extreme behavior. These patterns include deep depressions as well as the explosions into violence.

The moon's influence on your body chemistry may also be at the bottom of another moon belief. In the dark ages of medicine, there was a practice of "letting blood" from the veins of a sick person in the hope of restoring a proper balance for good health. Experience with that practice confirmed an earlier observation that bleeding would be easier to control during certain phases of the moon than at other times. Modern surgery is beginning to recognize the validity of this old belief. A careful review of hospital records has shown that hemorrhages are most likely to occur, and more difficult to control, during a Full Moon.

The moon's influence on blood chemistry must also account for the many beliefs in the moon's power over women. The menstrual cycle has long been linked to the monthly cycle of the moon around the earth. (We are going to take a special look at the moon's influence on women in Chapter 7.) The moon is also thought to affect amorous moods, ovulation, conception and birth. An

29

ancient belief has recently been revived which claims that the sex of an unborn child depends on the moon's sign of the zodiac on the day the child was conceived. Interestingly, the statistics available from the big cities are now used to help discover the truths behind these ancient tenets.

Perhaps the oldest moon beliefs which still enjoy an active following are the beliefs in the astrological significance of the moon's sign at your time of birth. Your natal moon sign provides the key to your inner character and personality. Here the moon is only one of several heavenly bodies whose positions in the zodiac help to determine your course through life. And yet, among all these bodies, the moon is believed to play a very significant role. We take a detailed look at moon astrology in Chapter 8.

As you can see, there are lunar theories to cover almost every phase of your life. We seem to be born by the moon, get sick by the moon, have accidents by the moon, and even die by the moon. Many of these theories are being examined with renewed interest by serious scientists. The search is on for more careful confirmation of observations which seem to link some important earthly event to the moon, and for more creative concepts which can suggest possible links between the moon and those events. Fortunately, space-age sciences are making new knowledge available which promises to throw a new light on these moon mysteries.

Let me tell you about some of these newer insights into how the moon can be affecting your life. We will begin by taking a closer look at the moon as it moves around the earth.

2
How the Moon Moves Around the Earth

Introduction

If you want to understand how the moon can affect your behavior, you have to understand how the moon can affect your environment. And that comes down to understanding how the moon moves around the earth.

Perhaps the best way to begin is to take a look at how the sun, earth and moon move around each other in space.

How Big, How Far?

It's very hard to get a feeling for the scale of our world from a set of numbers that give you the diameters and distances between the sun, earth and moon. Who can visualize a million miles, or even thousands of miles?

So, instead of using miles, I am going to show you how to use relative sizes and distances to build up your own images.

Let's start with the earth and the moon.

The earth is four times larger than the moon. If you

31

choose an object to represent the earth, you have to choose another object one-fourth that size to represent the moon.

Suppose you choose a basketball to represent the earth. That would be about one foot in diameter (12 inches). The moon would then have to be one-fourth that size, or about 3 inches. A tennis ball is about the right size. If you had chosen a 4-inch grapefruit to represent the earth, you would have to choose something like a one-inch plum to represent the moon.

Once you choose the objects to represent the earth and the moon, you then have to place the moon at an appropriate distance to represent its orbit around the earth. On the scale of the basketball-sized earth, you would have to place the tennis ball about ten paces away to represent the moon's distance from the earth. That's because the moon circles the earth at an average distance of about thirty "earth-diameters." For the one-foot basketball, thirty earth-diameters would come to 30 feet, or ten paces away. If you have trouble visualizing 30 feet, or ten paces, imagine five tall people laid head-to-toe between the basketball and the tennis ball.

And now for the sun. How big, and how far away? Let's look at it in terms of our basketball-sized earth.

Remember, starting from the basketball, you would have to walk ten paces before you reached the tennis ball that represented the moon. You would have to walk another two and a quarter miles to reach the sun! When you got there, the sun would be a large ball, about 100 feet high. That's because the sun is 100 times larger than the earth. A ten-story building is about 100 feet high.

Even on this scale it is hard to imagine the relative sizes and distances between the sun, earth and moon.

There is an interesting relationship between the sizes of the sun and the moon, and their distances from the earth. It helps to explain how the small moon blocks out the larger sun during a solar eclipse.

We just saw that the earth is four times larger than the moon, and the sun is 100 times larger than the earth. That means that the sun is 400 times larger than the moon. For some reason, the sun happens to be 400

32

times further away from us than the moon. This means that, even though it is 400 times larger its equally greater distance from us makes the sun appear to be about the same size as the moon. When the two bodies line up during a solar eclipse, the moon just about covers the sun.

While we are still talking about the relative sizes of things, a few more comparisons may give you an even better feel for the scale of our world.

Our atmosphere is an ocean of air that reaches to a height of approximately 100 miles. That would extend to about a quarter-inch from the surface of our basketball.

Those cloud-cover pictures you see on the TV weather reports are taken from satellites that are 20,000 miles from the earth. On our scale, the satellites would be specks, hovering over their stations, 30 inches from the basketball.

Our nearest planetary neighbor, Venus, would be found about a half mile away, while Pluto, our most distant neighbor in this solar system, would be about 85 miles away!

I have to change the scale a bit to round out your celestial picture. If the sun were a Ping-Pong ball in New York City, the nearest stars would be Ping-Pong balls located in Denver! No wonder it's so hard to believe that the stars can have an influence on us, here on earth.

The View from Earth

The earth has two important motions. It rotates on its axis once a day, giving us day and night. And it makes one complete revolution around the sun each year, giving us the seasons.

Most of us know that it is daytime on the side of the earth that faces the sun. And that when that side rotates away from the sun, it enters the earth's own shadow into night.

But do you remember what causes the annual change of the seasons? Even if I remind you that the earth's orbit is closer to the sun in winter than it is in the summer?

33

Sun Positions and the Four Seasons

Imagine that your head represents the earth. The earth's equator would be a horizontal plane passing through your head at eye level. (We won't worry about relative sizes here. All we want to see is how things seem to move around the earth. And where they are with respect to the equator.)

Now imagine yourself sitting on a chair in the middle of a large, empty room. Place the chair so that you are facing one of the corners of the room. Think of that corner as the home plate of a baseball diamond. Your chair would be on the pitcher's mound. The other corners of the room then become first base to your left, second base behind you, and third base on your right. I will give these corners different names in a little while. But for now we need the baseball diamond to get ourselves oriented.

We are going to follow the sun around the bases as it moves from season to season. These seasons are the ones you experience if you are in the Northern Hemisphere. The same sun positions cause the opposite seasons in the Southern Hemisphere. You will soon see why.

Let's begin with the first day of winter.

Place your left hand in front of you, pointing toward home plate. Now point your finger about 12 inches below eye level. That is the direction of the sun from the earth (your head) on December 22 each year. The sun is at its lowest point below eye level. That means that it is at its lowest point below the earth's equator.

Now move your outstretched arm toward your left, and slowly raise it until it is at eye level by the time it reaches first base. Notice that since your hand is now at eye level, the sun would be on the equator. You have just traced the path that the sun follows as it moves around the earth from December 22 to March 21. Its position at first base marks the first day of spring.

Let's now follow the sun into the next season. Continue moving your arm around toward second base, raising it slowly until it is about 12 inches above eye level when it finally gets to second base. You are now pointing toward the sun on June 22, the first day of sum-

34

mer. That's the highest point on the sun's path above the earth's equator.

As the sun moves on from summer to autumn, it falls from its highest point over second base until it is again at eye level when it reaches third base. That's the position of the sun on September 23, the first day of fall. The sun is again on the equator. But this time it is moving from above the equator to below the equator.

Let's complete the sun's annual trip around the earth. Bring your arm forward toward home plate, lowering it slowly so that it is again about 12 inches below eye level when it is back at the starting point. You are now back to the first day of winter, ready to start another year.

Now, while it's still fresh in your mind, let's review how the sun moves around the earth through each of the four seasons. The sun starts low at home plate (winter), slowly rises to eye level (the earth's equator) at first base (spring), continues to its highest point at second base (summer), falls back to eye level (equator) at third base (autumn) and then returns to its lowest point below the equator at home plate (winter, again).

Keep that image in mind. That's also the path followed by the moon as it moves around the earth each month. Well, almost.

What Causes the Seasons

Now that you see how the sun moves around the earth during the year, it is time to refresh your memory as to what causes the seasons. A picture will make it much easier for you to visualize this.

Figure 2-1A shows the positions of the sun on the first day of each of the four seasons. Remember, these are the seasons as experienced in the Northern Hemisphere. Notice that the sun is below the equator in winter and above it in summer, and that the sun is on the earth's equator at the start of spring and fall.

Figure 2-1B shows how sunlight and darkness cover the earth when the sun is below the equator. The darkness falls where the earth shadows itself from the sun's rays. You can see that when the sun is below the

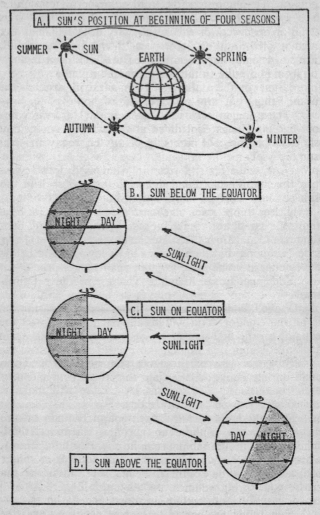

A. SUN'S POSITION AT BEGINNING OF FOUR SEASONS

SUMMER — SUN

EARTH — SPRING

AUTUMN

WINTER

B. SUN BELOW THE EQUATOR

NIGHT DAY

SUNLIGHT

C. SUN ON EQUATOR

NIGHT DAY

SUNLIGHT

SUNLIGHT

DAY NIGHT

D. SUN ABOVE THE EQUATOR

Fig. 2–1 How the Sun's Positions Cause the Seasons

36

equator, the Northern Hemisphere is covered by more shadow and less light, more so as you move north of the equator. The opposite is true of the Southern Hemisphere.

Look again at the Northern Hemisphere in Figure 2-1B. Whenever a point on the earth is in the shadowed area it is night. When that point moves into the lighted area it becomes day. You can see that as the earth turns on its axis, a point in the Northern Hemisphere will spend more time in the darkness than in the light and heat of the sun.

These longer nights and shorter days are the cause of winters. Things cool down as the warm days become shorter than the cool nights. To make matters worse, the sun's rays come in at shallower angles when they approach from below the equator. That spreads the same heat over a greater area, giving the earth less heat per square foot.

If you look again at Figure 2-1B you can see that things are reversed in the Southern Hemisphere. The days are longer than the nights, and the sun's rays arrive from more nearly overhead. That's why it is summer in the Southern Hemisphere when the sun is below the equator. You might remember it this way: "Summer follows the sun."

Figure 2-1C shows how things are when the sun is on the equator. You will recall that the sun is on the equator on the first day of spring (first base), and again at the beginning of autumn (third base). Notice how the sunlight covers the earth so that the areas of darkness and light are equal. That means that the nights and days are also equal.

These two days when the sun is on the equator are called the spring equinox, when the sun moves from the Southern Hemisphere up into the Northern Hemisphere, and the autumnal equinox (or fall equinox), when the sun moves from the Northern Hemisphere back down into the Southern Hemisphere. After the sun crosses the spring equinox the days get longer. After it crosses the fall equinox they get shorter.

Now follow the sun to its highest position above the equator (at second base) to see why it brings summer to the Northern Hemisphere. Figure 2-1D shows how the sun lights the earth when it is at its highest point. This time the sunlit areas are larger than the areas of darkness, and the days are therefore longer than the nights. They become longer yet, as you go to the higher latitudes. Also, since the sun's rays arrive from more nearly overhead, they deliver more energy per square foot to add to the heat of summer. So again we see that "Summer follows the sun."

The Concept of Moon Seasons

You just saw how the sun's position above or below the equator determines the length of the solar days, and how that determines the annual seasons.

You will soon see that the moon moves around the earth in a path similar to the one we traced out for the sun. If you replace the sun with the moon in Figure 2-1, you can see how the moon's positions with respect to the equator will determine how the areas of moonlight and shadows fall on the earth. As the earth rotates through these unequal areas of moonlight, it will cause unequal lengths of moon days and moon nights, just as it did with solar days and nights.

What this means is that the moon's monthly motion around the earth brings with it four "moon seasons" in the same way that the sun's yearly motion brings with it the four "solar seasons." In each case, the seasons are determined by the position of the sun or the moon with respect to the earth's equator.

There are two important differences between moon seasons and sun seasons. First, there is the matter of duration. Each season occupies one-fourth of an orbit. Since it takes 12 months for the sun to complete one orbit, each solar season equals 3 months. The moon completes one orbit in about a month. That means that each moon season lasts about one week.

The second difference between sun seasons and moon seasons has to do with what makes one season different from the others. In the case of sun seasons we are talking about changes in light and temperature, both of which are important environmental influences on life processes. In the case of the moon seasons, you will soon

38

see that the weekly changes of seasons bring with them changes in the gravitational forces, which in turn affect magnetic and electric fields. Recent studies are beginning to show how life processes are attuned to these changing fields.

So moon seasons, then, are seasons of "forces and fields," while sun seasons are seasons of "light and temperature." Both are important elements of our environment. And both depend on where the sun and the moon are with respect to the earth's equator. The question then is, how can you tell where the sun and moon are with respect to the earth's equator. The answer is, from the sun signs and the moon signs. Let's see why that is so.

Sun Signs and the Seasons

Let's go back to your chair, facing home plate. Visualize the path followed by the sun as it moved around the bases. That path lies in a plane that is tilted downward toward home plate and upward over second base. That plane, tilted at an angle of $23\frac{1}{2}$ degrees from the earth's equator, is called the ecliptic plane. The name comes from the fact that the eclipses occur only when the sun and moon are in that plane.

The sun and all its planets *seem* to move around the earth in orbits that lie in, or close to, the ecliptic plane. The moon's orbit is tilted about 5 degrees from the ecliptic plane. I will have more to say about the moon's oribit soon.

Ancient astronomers who watched the planets circle the earth had to develop a method for describing where a celestial object could be found along its path on the ecliptic plane. So they divided the 360-degree ecliptic path into twelve sectors. Then they named each sector after a group of stars that seemed to remain fixed in that sector.

Most of the fixed star groups, or constellations, were named after animals. And so the band of animals that circled the ecliptic path came to be known as the Little Zoo, or Zodiac. Each animal became a "sign" for its sector of the zodiac. When you wanted to describe where a

39

planet could be found, you identified the "sign of the zodiac" in which the planet happened to be at that time.

The sun moves through all twelve signs of the zodiac as it makes its yearly trip around the ecliptic. On any given date the sun can be found in a given sign. If you were born on a particular date, you can identify that date by the sign of the zodiac which the sun occupied on that date. These are the familiar "sun signs" of astrology. If you are a Capricorn, it means that the sun was in the sign of Capricorn on the day you were born. Most people, whether they are familiar with astrology or not, are familiar with their sun signs.

Not so with moon signs. Few people know their moon signs, or anything about moon signs. Your moon sign is the sign of the zodiac occupied by the moon on the day you were born. I'll show you how to find moon signs in Chapter 4. Then I'll show you how to use moon signs to learn more about how the moon may be influencing you.

But now let's see how the sun signs tell us the seasons of the year. We'll do that by assigning the appropriate signs of the zodiac to the four corners of our baseball diamond where each of the four seasons began.

You recall that we started at home plate on the first day of winter. Since the sun enters Capricorn on the first day of winter, we will rename home plate Capricorn, the Goat. On that date, around December 22, the sun reaches its lowest point below the equator. As it falls to that point and then starts to rise again, it seems to be standing still. That is, it seems to stand still with respect to its motion from the equator. That first day of Capricorn is called the winter solstice. Solstice means "sun stands still."

If you draw a line from the center of the earth to the sun when it enters Capricorn, the line would, come out of the earth's surface at the parallel of latitude 23½ degrees south of the equator. That latitude, a circle around the earth parallel to and below the equator, is called the Tropic of Capricorn. The sun is directly over the Tropic of Capricorn at noon on December 22. That's as far as it gets below the equator.

The Tropic of Capricorn cuts across the middle of

Australia, passes through lower Madagascar and then crosses South Africa near Pretoria. It then moves across the Atlantic to pass through the middle of South America. If you were in places like São Paulo, Brazil, or Antofagasta, Chile, you would be right on the Tropic of Capricorn.

Now let's move from winter to spring. That takes us to first base. That's where the sun's path crosses the equator as it moves from the Southern Hemisphere into the Northern Hemisphere on March 21. Remember, that's the day of the spring equinox. That point, where the sun crosses up through the equator, is defined as the first point of Aries, the Ram. Actually, because of a phenomenon called the precession of the equinoxes, the spring equinox now occurs a little earlier in the sign of Pisces. But, by agreement, the first day of spring is called Aries.

Aries is the first sign of the zodiac. The other signs of the zodiac, each occupying a 30-degree sector, are counted, starting from Aries as the first sector.

From now on, when you think of the sun's position on the first day of spring, you should see it at first base, coming up through the equator. Soon you will associate the first day of spring with the first sign of the zodiac, Aries.

Summer begins when the sun reaches its highest point above the equator, at second base. The sign of the zodiac at that position along the ecliptic is Cancer, the Crab. So, second base will be called Cancer from now on. Once again, as the sun changes its direction from rising to falling relative to the equator, it seems to stand still. The day the sun seems to stand still as it enters Cancer is called the summer solstice.

If you draw a line from the center of the earth to the sun in Cancer, it will emerge from the earth at a parallel of latitude that is 23½ degrees north of the equator. That parallel is called the Tropic of Cancer. The sun would be directly overhead at noon if you were standing on the Tropic of Cancer on the first day of summer on June 22.

The closest you can get to the Tropic of Cancer in the United States is at Key West, Florida. Key West is at a latitude of 24½ degrees north. That's one degree higher

41

than the sun's maximum climb to 23½ degrees above the equator. You would have to go further south, to a place like Havana, Cuba, to be able to see the sun directly overhead. The tropic of Cancer crosses just over Havana, and continues across the middle of Mexico before crossing the Pacific, passing a few degrees north of Hawaii. It then touches Formosa and continues across southern China, northern India, and finally cuts across Africa in the Sahara Desert.

After the sun reaches its highest point over the Tropic of Cancer, it again falls toward the equator, crossing it at the fall equinox to mark the beginning of autumn. The sun would be at third base when it falls below the equator into the Southern Hemisphere. The sign of the zodiac corresponding with the fall equinox at third base is Libra, the Scales (not an animal this time). Libra is on the opposite side of the ecliptic from Aries, which marked the spring equinox.

After passing through the fall equinox, the sun continues to fall below the equator until it again reaches its lowest point at Capricorn (home plate). A year has passed, and another winter is about to begin.

The four signs of the zodiac that mark the beginning of the four seasons serve as reference points against which the other signs can be remembered as well. Perhaps this listing will help you retain the visualization you just went through:

Home Plate —Capricorn —Winter
First Base —Aries —Spring
Second Base —Cancer —Summer
Third Base —Libra —Fall

You can find a complete listing of the signs of the zodiac in Table 1. The table shows the dates during which the sun can be found in each of the signs, and the seasons associated with them. You can also see the sun's position with respect to the equator when it is in any of the signs.

If you consult different lists for the dates of the signs of the zodiac, you may find that some dates differ by a day or so, in either direction. That's because the

42

TABLE 1 - SIGNS OF THE ZODIAC
THEIR DATES
AND THEIR SEASONS

DATE	SIGN		SEASONS	ORBIT POSITION
MAR 21 - - APR 20	ARIES	♈	SPRING EQUINOX	ON EQUATOR (RISING)
APR 21 - - MAY 21	TAURUS	♉	EARLY SPRING	ABOVE EQUATOR
MAY 22 - - JUN 21	GEMINI	♊	LATE SPRING	ABOVE EQUATOR
JUN 22 - - JUL 22	CANCER	♋	SUMMER SOLSTICE	HIGHEST POINT
JUL 23 - - AUG 23	LEO	♌	EARLY SUMMER	ABOVE EQUATOR
AUG 24 - - SEP 22	VIRGO	♍	LATE SUMMER	ABOVE EQUATOR
SEP 23 - - OCT 23	LIBRA	♎	FALL EQUINOX	ON EQUATOR (FALLING)
OCT 24 - - NOV 22	SCORPIO	♏	EARLY FALL	BELOW EQUATOR
NOV 23 - - DEC 21	SAGITTARIUS	♐	LATE FALL	BELOW EQUATOR
DEC 22 - - JAN 20	CAPRICORN	♑	WINTER SOLSTICE	LOWEST POINT
JAN 21 - - FEB 19	AQUARIUS	♒	EARLY WINTER	BELOW EQUATOR
FEB 20 - - MAR 20	PISCES	♓	LATE WINTER	BELOW EQUATOR

Table 1 Signs of the Zodiac, Their Dates and Their Seasons

43

earth's speed around the sun isn't constant. And, sometimes it takes a little longer (or shorter) time to reach the equinox or solstice positions. It all depends on the year.

Unfortunately, you can't use Table 1 to find where the moon is in its orbit along the zodiac. For one thing, the moon makes over a dozen orbits in one year, and so it will be in one sign of the zodiac on a dozen different dates. Furthermore, since the moon's period does not fit evenly into the solar calendar, the moon would be in that same sign on different dates in the following year. As I have said, I will show you an easy way to find moon signs in Chapter 4.

Once you know the moon's sign you can use Table 1 to see when the moon enters its different moon seasons or when the moon is above or below the equator. Remember, just as the sun's position with respect to the equator tells you the sun seasons, so too the moon's position with respect to the equator tells you the moon seasons. Equally important, the moon's position with respect to the equator tells you how its gravitational pull changes. You will be able to see this more easily after we take a closer look at how the moon orbits around the earth.

The Moon's Orbit—"Tilt!"

The motions of the moon are so complicated that you can't describe them completely. You always have to leave something out. I am going to leave out many things so we can focus on the few that are essential to our purposes: those moon motions that cause the important periodic changes in your environment. Let's begin by seeing how the moon orbits around the earth.

You remember that the moon's orbit lies almost in the ecliptic plane. You saw that the ecliptic plane was tilted 23½ degrees from the equator. Down toward Capricorn (home plate), and up toward Cancer (second base). The tilt is slowly turning around the zodiac. But you won't notice that because it will take 26,000 years to go around one time.

The moon's orbit is tilted 5 degrees from the eclip-

44

tic plane. And that tilt is also slowly turning around the zodiac. However, in this case, it takes only 18.6 years to go around one time. That is, 18 years, 7 months and 6 days. You may not notice this motion either, unless you begin looking for 18.6-year cycles in your life.

Let's try to visualize this 5-degree tilt of the moon's orbit as it slowly circles the zodiac.

You recall how the sun moved around you in your chair as it traced out the ecliptic plane. It was low in Capricorn (home plate), over your head in Cancer (second base), then down again to eye level in Libra (third base). You also saw what 23½ degrees looked like, when you pointed about 12 inches below your eye level, toward Capricorn.

Imagine now that you are in your chair, wearing a rather broad-brimmed hat, with its circular brim straight out around your head. Something like the hat that Smokey the Bear wears. The edge of the hat will represent the path followed by the moon.

Now reach up and tilt the hat forward on your foreahead so that the brim lies in the ecliptic plane. This will be the starting position for tilting the moon's orbit away from the ecliptic plane. I will describe four positions of the moon's orbital plane as they would appear after four consecutive intervals of time, each 4.65 years, or one-fourth of the 18.6-year cycle.

For the first position, tilt your hat brim slightly below the ecliptic plane at Capricorn. The tilt should be 5 degrees below the ecliptic. You can find that direction by pointing your finger about 16 inches below your eye level, toward the Capricorn corner of the room. (When you pointed to 23½ degrees, you pointed 12 inches below your eye level.)

With your hat brim pointed below the ecliptic in Capricorn, the moon's orbit is at its maximum angle from the earth's equator. That happens every 18.6 years. The last time that happened was from October 1967 to April 1969. It will be that way again from May 1986 to November 1987. At these times the orbit carries the moon 28½ degrees from the equator as it passes through Capricorn or Cancer. Remember, as you push the front of your hat below Capricorn, the back of your hat rises above Cancer. That 5-degree rise is also added to the 23½ degrees of the ecliptic plane at Cancer.

If the sun moved that far from the equator, it would cause major changes in the sun seasons. That's because if the sun moved further north or south of the equator than it does now (23½ degrees), it would make the summer days longer and the winter days shorter than they are now.

You can see then, that during these years when the moon's orbit is tilted below Capricorn, the moon moves further from the equator, causing an increase in the "severity" of the monthly moon seasons because the moon days and moon nights become longer or shorter than at other times.

Let's go now to the next position of the tilted moon orbit. First, return your hat brim to its starting position in the ecliptic plane. Now, cock your hat so that the brim is low over your right ear and high over your left ear. When it is in this position the moon's orbit is below the ecliptic at Libra (third base) and above it at Aries (first base). In each case, by the same 5 degrees. To find that 5 degrees, point about 3 inches below your eye level, toward third base.

While it is tilted below Libra, the moon's orbit passes through the ecliptic plane at Capricorn and Cancer. That means that the severity of the moon seasons would be the same as the sun seasons, since the moon moves no higher or lower from the equator than the sun does, when it is in Capricorn or Cancer. This is the position of the moon's orbit as it was from November 1953 to April 1955, and again from June 1972 to December 1973. (Don't try to remember these times of the orbit's tilt, since I will give you a table [Table 6] to find them all in Chapter 4.)

The third position of the orbit is opposite to the first one. Here, your hat brim should be tilted so that it is slightly below the ecliptic at Cancer (second base). That would bring the front of your hat slightly above the ecliptic at Capricorn (home plate). If you can visualize this position you should be able to see that the moon's orbit now makes its shallowest tilt with respect to the earth's equator.

46

Try to see the moon's orbit below the ecliptic at Cancer. The ecliptic is 23½ degrees above the equator at Cancer. So, the moon's orbit, 5 degrees below that, would be only 18½ degrees above the equator.

When the moon moves in such a shallow orbit, the moon days and moon nights are nearly the same length. And so the monthly moon seasons will be much the same, all of them "mild."

The last time the moon was in such a shallow orbit was from February 1977 to July 1978. The time before that was from June 1958 to December 1959. Do you remember if there was anything special about those years in your life? Were they periods of intense activity or periods of the passive doldrums? Did they mark great beginnings or drawn-out endings? Sometimes you can spot interesting correlations between important periods in your life and the tilt of the moon's orbit in its 18.6-year cycle.

But let's move on now to complete the picture by seeing what happens 4.65 years later. That's 4 years, 7 months and 24 days later. The moon's orbit (the hat brim) is now tilted 5 degrees below the ecliptic at Aries (first base) and 5 degrees above the ecliptic at Libra (third base). Here again the moon's orbit passes through the ecliptic at Capricorn and Cancer. Which means that the moon seasons have the same "severity" as the sun seasons.

The moon's orbit was tilted below the ecliptic at Aries from February 1963 to August 1964. It will be that way again from October 1981 to March 1983.

While it is still fresh in your memory, let's review how the moon's orbit tilts around the zodiac once every 18.6 years. Hat brim below the ecliptic in Capricorn, then below the ecliptic in Libra, then Cancer, and Aries before finally returning to the starting position below Capricorn.

When the orbit is tilted below Capricorn, the monthly moon seasons are the most extreme. When it is tilted below Cancer, 9.3 years later, the monthly moon seasons are at their mildest.

I want to emphasize something that I hope you have already noticed for yourself. Regardless of whether it is tilted 18½, 23½ or 28½ degrees, the moon's orbit

47

carries the moon furthest from the equator when it is near Capricorn and again when it is near Cancer. And, the moon is nearest to the equator when it is in Aries and Libra. In other words, you can tell where the moon is with respect to the equator if you know the moon sign. Since the moon sign tells you the moon's position with respect to the equator, it tells you the moon season!

Once you understand this relationship between moon sign and moon seasons, you can use Table 1 to find the moon seasons from the corresponding signs of the zodiac. For example, if the moon sign is between Libra and Capricorn, it is moon autumn. What would the moon season be if the moon sign is in a sign between Capricorn and Aries? If you know your sun signs, you would recognize that it is the winter season (between December 22 and March 21). When the moon sign is between Capricorn and Aries it tells you that it is moon winter.

The effect of the moon's slowly tilting orbit is to introduce an 18.6-year cycle in the severity of moon seasons. I have provided a table in Chapter 4 (Table 6) to help you find the severity of the moon seasons during any year from March 1893 to December 2001.

Now that you know something about how the moon's orbit is oriented in space around the earth, let's take a look at how the moon moves along this orbit as it circles the earth once a month.

As the Moon Turns—Phases of the Moon

The moon moves around the earth in the same direction that the sun seems to move around the earth. However, the moon moves much faster around its orbit, making a little over twelve trips during the time the sun makes only one. I'm not talking about their daily motion across the skies. That motion is caused by the earth's rotation on its axis once a day. I am talking about the monthly trip of the moon and the yearly trip of the sun around the spinning earth.

As the moon overtakes and passes the sun each month, it appears to go through a series of changing shapes, known as the phases of the moon. Let's take a

48

closer look at these to see why they appear and what they can tell us about the moon's position, relative to the sun.

We can begin, again in the chair in the middle of your imaginary baseball diamond, facing home plate (Capricorn). This time, imagine a bright lamp at Capricorn. That will be the sun. Now imagine that you are holding a grapefruit to represent the moon. We will forget about relative sizes for now. The grapefruit is the right size to help you visualize how the light of the sun falls on the moon as it moves around the earth each month.

Let's start a monthly orbit with the moon in Capricorn. It will be a little above or below the sun, depending on the moon's tilt with respect to the ecliptic plane that year. In any case, the light from the lamp will fall on the side of the grapefruit that is facing away from you, toward the lamp. The side facing you would be dark. Whenever the moon is in the same direction as the sun, regardless of where the sun is in the zodiac, the moon is dark on the side facing the earth. This is called the *New Moon*. It is the starting point from which the other phases are "counted."

The New Moon is always in the same sign of the zodiac as the sun sign, since the moon is then in the same direction as the sun. Since they are in the same sign of the zodiac, the moon season will always be the same as the sun season during a New Moon.

You have to wait a couple of days after a New Moon before it becomes visible again. You then see it as a thin crescent near the horizon, just after sunset. If you move your grapefruit toward first base you will see this thin crescent of light forming on the right side of the grapefruit. Notice that the shape curves out to your right as the moon begins its new orbit.

When your grapefruit gets to Aries (first base), the half that faces the sun is bright, while the opposite side is dark. If you turn in your chair to look at the moon at first base, you will see that its right half is bright while the left half is dark. This is the way the moon always looks when it is one-quarter of the way through its or-

49

bit, starting from a New Moon. That "half moon" shape is the *First Quarter Moon*. The next time you see a half moon with its round part to your right, you will know that you are looking at a First Quarter Moon.

Unfortunately, the names of the moon's phases are a bad combination of names for moon shapes and names for moon positions. But everyone seems to overcome the initial confusion, once they learn which shapes go with which positions.

It takes about 7 or 8 days for the moon to move from its position at New Moon to its position at First Quarter. That would be from Capricorn to Aries in our example. By the way, don't get the idea from this example that the First Quarter Moon always occurs in Aries! The only reason this happened here was that we started the orbit with the sun in Capricorn, and Aries is one-quarter of the way around the zodiac from Capricorn. If the sun were in Aries to begin with, we would have had a New Moon when the moon got to Aries. It would then have to move to Cancer before it reached its First Quarter. That's because Cancer is one-quarter of the way around the zodiac from Aries. So you see, the moon's sign doesn't tell you the moon's phase. That is, not unless you happen to know where the sun is at that time.

Let's continue to follow the moon around in its orbit, keeping the sun where it is, in Capricorn. When the moon reaches Cancer (second base), it is on the opposite side of the earth from the sun in Capricorn. Hold up your grapefruit in Cancer and look at it. You are now looking at the legendary *Full Moon*. This is the same side of the moon that you always look at. The side that always faces the earth. But now, it is also facing the sun. What you see is the full face of the moon as it reflects the sunlight.

The Full Moon, you notice, is only halfway through its orbit. Full Moons appear about 14 or 15 days after the New Moon. They always appear in the opposite sign of the zodiac in which the sun can be found at that time. That should tell you something about the moon season during a Full Moon. Moon seasons are always the opposite of the sun seasons during a Full Moon!

50

While we are talking about Full Moons and seasons, let me show you why the Full Moon rides high in the sky during winter, and low in the sky during summer.

During the winter the sun is low in the sign of Capricorn (home plate). The Full Moon is always in the opposite sign of the zodiac. So the Full Moon would be in the sign of Cancer during the winter. The moon's orbit is at its highest point in the sky at that time.

In summer, when the sun is in Cancer, the Full Moon would be in the opposite sign of Capricorn. That is the lowest point on the moon's orbit, so the moon would be at its lowest position in the sky during summer. It all becomes easy when you can visualize how the moon moves around the earth.

About 7 or 8 days after the Full Moon, the moon is three-quarters of the way through its orbit. You can visualize that position if you move your grapefruit over to third base, into Libra. If you turn now to face the moon you will see that the left side, facing the sun at home plate, is bright while the right side is dark. This is just the opposite of the way it looked when you saw it at First Quarter.

Whenever you see a half moon with its bright side to your left, you will know that you are looking at the Third Quarter Moon. It is also called the *Last Quarter Moon* because it has one more quarter to go to complete its orbit.

After the Third (or Last) Quarter Moon, the Moon moves on to face the sun again for the next New Moon. But the sun won't be there! At least it won't be where it was at the start of the last orbit. While the moon was out on its orbit, the sun was also moving on its annual trip around the zodiac. In fact, the sun moves through one sign of the zodiac during the time it takes for the moon to make one trip around the earth. It takes 29½ days for the moon to catch up with the sun, from one New Moon to the next New Moon. That's why calendars show 29 days between some New Moons and 30 days between others. If you do the arithmetic, you will find that over the year it averages out to 29½ days from New Moon to New Moon.

51

Other Ways to Describe Moon Phases

The moon's shape changes a little bit each day, from one New Moon to the next. You might say that there is a different shape, or moon phase, for each day of the month. But you would be hard pressed to describe how the shape differs from one day to the next.

One way to identify these daily phases is simply to indicate the number of days since the last New Moon. In fact, almanacs do just that. The number of days since the last New Moon is called the "moon's age." The New Moon has an age of 0 days. The First Quarter Moon has an age of 7 days. The Full Moon has an age of 15 days, and the Last Quarter, an age of 22 days.

There is still another way to describe the moon's phases. It involves giving names to four other shapes by which the moon can be recognized as it moves between the four positions which define the four basic phases. Figure 2-2 shows you these intermediate shapes and their positions along the moon's orbit around the earth.

The shapes shown in Figure 2-2 are those you would see for a few days during each of the phases they represent. If you can recognize these shapes, you should be able to tell the moon's age to within a couple of days. The moon's ages corresponding with the eight phases are shown in the figure.

The first four phases are those during which the moon's shape grows larger. These are the "waxing phases." The last four phases are those in which the moon's shape becomes smaller. These are the "waning phases." Notice that the bright sides of the moon are toward the right during the waxing phases, and toward the left during the waning phases.

Moon Phases, Signs and Seasons

Let me point out something significant about what you can learn from the moon's phases. Since the moon's phase depends on the difference between the sun's position and the moon's position along their paths, the *Moon's phase tells you the difference between the sun sign and the moon sign*. If you know the sun sign, the moon

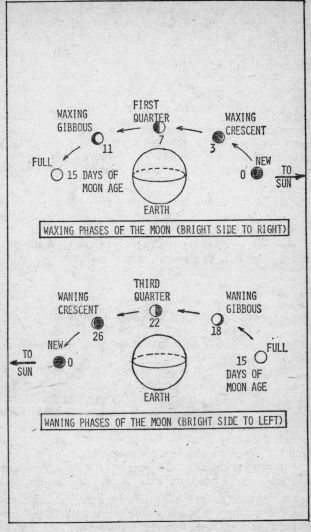

WAXING GIBBOUS FIRST QUARTER WAXING CRESCENT

11 7 3

FULL 15 DAYS OF MOON AGE 0 NEW TO SUN

EARTH

WAXING PHASES OF THE MOON (BRIGHT SIDE TO RIGHT)

WANING CRESCENT THIRD QUARTER WANING GIBBOUS

26 22 18

TO SUN NEW 0 15 DAYS OF MOON AGE FULL

EARTH

WANING PHASES OF THE MOON (BRIGHT SIDE TO LEFT)

Fig. 2–2 The Recognizable Shapes of the Moon's Phases

53

phase can tell you the moon sign. In fact, the tables and charts in Chapter 4 do that for you.

You recall that the signs of the zodiac correspond with the seasons. Since the moon's phase tells you the difference between the sun signs and the moon signs, the moon's phase tells you the difference between the sun's season and the moon's season:

When the Sun Season Is:	Moon Seasons will be as shown during the phases:		
	New Moon	First Quarter	Full Moon	Last Quarter
Winter	Winter	Spring	Summer	Fall
Spring	Spring	Summer	Fall	Winter
Summer	Summer	Fall	Winter	Spring
Fall	Fall	Winter	Spring	Summer

When you begin your search for the influence of the moon in your life, you may find that certain combinations of sun and moon seasons are more significant for you than others, especially as they relate to the seasons of your birth, or the birth of your companions.

Postscript

I said earlier that we had to leave out many things in our description of the moon's orbit. Let me at least tell you some of the more important things that were left out.

Perhaps the most important was the omission of any mention of apogee and perigee. These are the points of furthest and closest approach to the earth of the moon's noncirculâr orbit, respectively. The moon moves fastest when it is closest at perigee, and slowest when it passes through the apogee point. The moon's gravitational pull is much stronger at perigee than at apogee.

A line connecting the apogee and perigee points (apsides) will rotate once every nine years in the plane of the orbit. That moves the perigee point into different signs of the zodiac over the years. However, this line also "oscillates" back and forth with a period of 31.81 days, because of monthly changes in the eccentricity of the moon's orbit. This variation is called evection. The ef-

54

fect of all this is that the moon speeds up and slows down at different rates in each of the four weeks from one perigee to the next.

Another factor that affects the moon's speed in its orbit is related to the moon's phases. The sun's pull on the moon is different in each quadrant of the moon phase cycle. The result is that the moon moves faster from the Last Quarter to the New Moon, and slower from the New Moon to the First Quarter. It again speeds up from the First Quarter to the Full Moon, and slows down from the Full Moon to the Last Quarter. These speed variations may play some important roles in the effect of the moon on your fields.

You should also know that the periods of the moon's various cycles are average values taken over many cycles. For example, the time between New Moons can vary from 27 to 30 days throughout the year. Yet, on the average, that period is 29.53 days. In the same way, the time for the moon to move once around the zodiac is an average of 27.32 days, and to go from one perigee to the next is 27.55 days. The time between crossing of the nodes is 27.21 days.

But let's move on now to see how the changing positions of the moon can affect you by the way it changes your environment.

3
How the Moon Gets to You

Introduction

When you finish this chapter you won't be wondering anymore about whether or not the moon can have an effect on your life. Instead, you will be wondering about which of its many influences are affecting you today. And of course I intend to help you find out.

You just saw how the moon's phase tells you where the moon is with respect to the sun. And how the moon's sign tells you where the moon is with respect to the earth's equator. Now I want to show you how these changing positions of the moon can bring about important changes in your environment.

All the important elements of your environment depend on the actions of two physical forces of nature: gravity and electromagnetic energy. Most of us recognize gravity as the force of attraction between two bodies. Today we know that the moon's gravity is the force that pulls the tides. But few of us can imagine how the moon's pull can have anything to do with the way we feel. Yet it does!

"Electromagnetic energy" is a broad term that includes radio waves, heat energy (infrared), light energy, ultraviolet, X rays, cosmic rays, and higher energies from space. These are all related by the fact that they arise from the vibrations of electric fields and magnetic fields which are exchanging energy between them. Electromagnetic energies differ from each other by the difference in the frequencies of their vibrations. Light energy is at a higher frequency than infrared heat waves, which in turn are at a higher frequency than radio waves.

Electromagnetic energies have been radiated by the sun and other stars since the beginning of time. It is only recently that technology has revealed the common characteristics of these energies and allowed us to observe them and their effects. As with gravity, these basic energies play important roles in creating your environment and therefore in affecting your life. We will look at these effects later in this chapter.

Right now I want to show you how the changing moon positions bring about important changes in the gravity and electromagnetic energies on earth. And how you can use the moon's phase and moon signs to tell you the status of those changing forces.

Gravity Cycles

Everything on the earth is pulled in a gravitational tug of war betwen the earth, sun and moon. But it's no contest. The earth is the big winner. When it comes to gravity, size is important. But distance is even more important. The closer two bodies are to each other, the stronger is the pull of gravity between them. Since we are on the earth, its pull on us is by far the strongest. The earth's gravity holds us to its surface with a force that is over nine million times stronger than the pull of the moon trying to lift us from that surface. The pull of the sun, for all its massive size, is only half as strong as the moon's because it is so much farther away from us.

Yet, these seemingly trivial gravitational forces of the sun and the moon are sufficient to raise the land, water and atmosphere in daily tides that are measured in inches, feet and miles, respectively! Few of us are

57

aware of land tides or tides in the atmosphere which affect our weather. But almost everyone has seen an incoming or an outgoing ocean tide.

The laws of gravitation help to explain why there are two high tides each day, and why tides run higher during Full Moons and New Moons. And why there are cycles in the tides with periods of hours, days, weeks, months, years and decades. It all comes down to the fact that the tidal forces depend on the time of day, the phase of the moon and the moon's sign. Let's take a closer look at how this works.

The moon's pull is strongest when it is closest to you—straight up over your head. That direction is called the zenith. The opposite direction is called the nadir. The easiest way to see how the pull of the moon varies throughout the day is to see where it is with respect to your zenith and your nadir.

As the earth rotates on its axis each day, the moon will come up over the eastern horizon. That would be the moonrise. If you are in the United States, the moon comes up in the southeast. The further south the moon is from your latitude, the further south it will be when it rises. Each month the moon is furthest south of the equator when it is in the sign of Capricorn. Conversely, it is furthest north of the equator when it is in the sign of Cancer. It would therefore be closer to your latitude when it is in Cancer.

If you point your right hand toward the moon as it rises, and your left hand straight up toward your zenith, the angle between your arms will show you how far the moon is from your zenith. The closer the moon comes to your zenith, the smaller the angle becomes. At moonrise, and again at moonset, that angle is the largest of the day. That tells you that the moon pulls on you with its weakest force at moonrise and again at moonset.

Now keep pointing to the moon as it continues to rise and move across the sky. It will remain at a constant distance to the south of you as it crosses from its moonrise in the southeast to its moonset in the southwest. When the moon reaches the midheaven, halfway between moonrise and moonset, the angle between your arms becomes

58

as small as it will get on that day. That's as close as the moon will come to being overhead at your zenith.

When the sun reaches the midheaven, between sunrise and sunset, it is noon. In the same way we can say that when the moon is at the midheaven, between moonrise and moonset, it is *moon noon*. The moon is closest to your zenith when it is moon noon. That's when you feel the strongest pull of the moon.

Before going on I have to explain something that is often very confusing. Why is it that there are two high tides each day on opposite sides of the earth? Some of you may have read that the moon pulls the earth away from the water on the far side of the earth. Not so. The answer involves another force besides gravity One that is always pointed away from the direction of the moon. Let me explain.

The moon doesn't revolve around the earth! The moon and the earth revolve around each other each month. They are on opposite sides of a common center, called a barycenter. As they revolve around this center, the earth experiences an outward force, away from the center of rotation. This outward force is called a centrifugal force. The word *centrifugal* means to flee from the center.

Since the moon is always on the opposite side of that center of rotation, the centrifugal force on the earth is always in the direction away from the moon! This is not the centrifugal force of the earth's daily rotation. It is the centrifugal force of the earth's monthly rotation around the barycenter, with the moon on the other side of that center.

But that force doesn't move the earth away from the moon. That's because the moon's gravitational force just balances the centrifugal force. At least that's what happens when you add up the forces all over the earth. The centrifugal force has the same strength everywhere on earth. And it always points away from the moon. However, on the side of the earth that faces the moon, the gravitational force toward the moon is stronger than the centrifugal force away from it. The net force is therefore toward the moon. When the moon is closest to your zenith

59

you feel the strongest pull of the moon's gravitational force.

At the same time, on the other side of the earth, the gravitational force is weaker than the centrifugal force, causing a net force directed away from the moon. Therefore, if you are on the opposite side of the earth when the moon is closest to your nadir, you will feel the maximum pull of the centrifugal force.

These pulls are equal on both sides of the earth. They balance each other out, which is why the earth and the moon remain together.

The only thing you need to remember about all this is that you will feel the moon's strongest pull when it is nearest to your zenith, at moon noon. And again, about 12 hours later, when the moon is nearest your nadir, at moon midnight.

The Daily Double (or, the Diurnal Inequality)

There's more to this story of the two strongest pulls of the day. Sometimes the pull at moon noon is stronger than the pull at moon midnight. Later in the month, it is the other way around. It all depends on the moon sign. When the moon is in Aries or Libra, the two pulls have the same strength. In the spring and summer signs, when the moon is above the equator, the pull at moon noon is stronger than the pull at moon midnight. When the moon is below the equator, in the fall and winter signs, it is just the opposite.

This means that the daily cycle of increasing and decreasing gravitational force, from moonrise to moonset, also has a monthly cycle superimposed on it. This monthly cycle, which depends on the moon sign, determines the range of values through which the force of gravity will vary during the day. It is responsible for the difference in the height of successive high tides. This difference is called the diurnal inequality. (*Diurnal* means daily.)

I want to show you how the moon sign can tell you the status of this daily inequality of moon forces. In your search to track down the moon's influence on you, you will want to know something about how the moon's force is changing through a day of special interest to you.

Remember that the moon's pull on you is strongest when it is closest to your zenith, and again when it is closest to your nadir. The closer it is to either one, the stronger the pull you feel.

Imagine that the moon is in Capricorn. Let's say that it is 20 degrees below the equator, as it would be in 1980. Also, let's say that you are in New York City, at a latitude of 40 degrees north of the equator. That means that your zenith lies along a line pointing away from the earth at an angle of 40 degrees north of the equator. Your nadir, straight down below your feet, through the center of the earth, would lie along a line coming out of the earth at 40 degrees *south* of the equator.

Now imagine that it is moon noon. The moon is on your side of the earth, and there is a 60-degree angle between your zenith and a line pointing to the moon. (Your zenith is 40 degrees north and the moon is 20 degrees south.) The pull of the moon would then be whatever force is produced by the moon at that 60-degree angle.

Twelve hours later the earth turns you away from the moon. It would then be moon midnight for you. The moon is still 20 degrees below the equator, because it is still in Capricorn. Your nadir, which points 40 degrees south of the equator, is now only 20 degrees away from the moon. That smaller angle produces a much stronger force than the 60-degree angle did at your zenith at moon noon. Remember, the closer the moon is to your zenith or nadir, the stronger is its force on you.

So you can see that when the moon is in Capricorn, you feel a stronger pull at moon midnight than you do at moon noon. It would be just the opposite when the moon enters the sign of Cancer, about two weeks later.

The moon's force at moonrise and moonset is also affected by the moon sign. The force is weakest at moonrise and moonset because your zenith and nadir are turned furthest from the moon at those times. However, as the moon comes closer to your latitude, these weak

61

forces become stronger. Since the moon is closest to your latitude when it reaches Cancer (if you are above the 30th parallel), the forces at moonrise and moonset are their strongest at that time of the month.

You won't have to figure out all these relationships between the moon signs and their effects on the daily pull of the moon. They are summarized in Table 2.

Table 2, Moonsigns and the Daily Inequality, shows the relative strength of the moon's pull at moonrise and moonset and at moon noon and moon midnight, during each of the moon signs. The moon signs are shown along with their moon seasons. The numerical values in the table represent the relative changes from a minimum force to a maximum force, on a scale of 1 to 5, respectively. The $(+)$ and $(-)$ notations after each number show whether the force is increasing $(+)$ or decreasing $(-)$ during that moon sign.

The last column in the table shows how the difference between the moon noon force and the moon midnight force varies with the moon signs. Notice that there is no difference between moon noon and moon midnight forces when the moon is in Aries or Libra. But there is a maximum daily inequality between them when the moon is in Cancer or Capricorn.

You may find that certain behavior seems to correlate with these changes in the daily inequality of the moon's pull. This table can be used to help you track down the correlations between changes in daily behavior and changes in the daily inequality.

I haven't yet told you how you can tell when it is moonrise or moon noon. If you believe the song, "I have the sun in the morning and the moon at night," you may be surprised by what's coming next.

Risings and Settings—Noons and Midnights

As you stand on the rotating earth facing east, there comes a moment each day when the sun comes up over the eastern horizon. That is sunrise. If there is a New Moon that day, that will also be the moment when the moon rises. That's because the New Moon is lined up

62

MOON SIGNS AND THE DAILY INEQUALITY					
MOON SIGN	MOON SEASON	RELATIVE STRENGTH AT			DAILY INEQUAL
		MOONRISE -MOONSET	MOON NOON	MOON MIDN	
♈ ARIES	SPRING EQUINOX	3(+)	3(+)	3(-)	NONE
♉ TAURUS	EARLY SPRING	4(+)	4(+)	2(-)	2(+)
♊ GEMINI	LATE SPRING	5(+)	5(+)	1(-)	4(+)
♋ CANCER	SUMMER SOLSTICE	MAX	MAX	MIN	MAX
♌ LEO	EARLY SUMMER	5(-)	5(-)	1(+)	4(-)
♍ VIRGO	LATE SUMMER	4(-)	4(-)	2(+)	2(-)
♎ LIBRA	FALL EQUINOX	3(-)	3(-)	3(+)	NONE
♏ SCORPIO	EARLY FALL	2(-)	2(-)	4(+)	2(+)
♐ SAGITT.	LATE FALL	1(-)	1(-)	5(+)	4(+)
♑ CAPRICORN	WINTER SOLSTICE	MIN	MIN	MAX	MAX
♒ AQUARIUS	EARLY WINTER	1(+)	1(+)	5(-)	4(-)
♓ PISCES	LATE WINTER	2(+)	2(+)	4(-)	2(-)

(+) INCREASING FORCE   (-) DECREASING FORCE

Table 2   Moon Signs and the Daily Inequality

63

with the sun and would come up over the horizon at the same time. Therefore, during a New Moon, moonrise occurs at the same time as sunrise.

But what about the moonrise when the moon is at its First Quarter? You will recall from Chapter 2 that a First Quarter Moon is one-quarter of the way further along the zodiac from the sun's position. The earth's rotation takes you once around the zodiac each day. Therefore it will take the earth a quarter of a day to turn from the sun's position to the moon's position at the First Quarter. That means that moonrise occurs six hours after sunrise when the moon is at First Quarter.

And what about a Full Moon? When does it rise?

Full Moons are halfway around the zodiac, opposite the position of the sun. And so it would take half a day for the earth to turn from the sun to the Full Moon. The moon would just be coming up on the eastern horizon as the sun was setting on the western horizon. It must have been the Full Moon that inspired the words to that song. Still, most people continue to think that the moon comes out only at night.

A Third Quarter Moon is three-quarters of the way around the zodiac ahead of the sun. Three-quarters of a day would take you from a 6 A.M. sunrise to midnight (18 hours later). Therefore, a Third Quarter Moon rises at midnight.

So, the time of moonrise depends on the phase of the moon. Moon noon occurs about six hours after moonrise. Moonset is about six hours after moon noon, and moon midnight about six hours after that. You won't have to remember all this because I have put it all into a chart (Fig. 4–2) for you in Chapter 4. It gives you the times for moonrise, moon noon, etc., for each day of the moon's phases. There are corrections for moon sign as well. Remember that the sun comes up earlier and sets later during the spring and summer months. When the moon is in those spring and summer signs it also rises earlier and sets later. Also, since the moonrise and moonset depend on how far the moon is from your latitude, there are corrections for your latitude as well.

These times of moonrise and moon noons will help

you track down how the daily changes in the moon's gravitational forces may be affecting you. But there are other, longer-term changes in the gravitational forces that will also be of interest. These come about as the moon and the sun change their distances from us and from each other during the month and during the year. Let's take a look at some of these longer cycles in the forces of gravity that tug at each of your cells.

Gravity and Moon Phase

I said earlier that the sun pulls on you in the same way that the moon pulls on you. But you don't feel them as separate forces, even though the moon's pull is twice as strong as the sun's pull. Instead, you feel a single force that depends on where the sun and moon are with respect to each other. That means that the combined force depends on the moon's phase. Let's look at how these two forces are combined during the month.

You will remember, when we talked about the two high tides each day, that the moon's pull is strongest on both sides of the earth, along a line that passes through the moon and the earth. The closer that moon-earth line is to your zenith-nadir line, the stronger is the force that you feel from the moon.

In the same way, the sun's pull is strongest on both sides of the earth along a line that passes through the sun and the earth. The sun's gravity pulls toward the sun on the day side of the earth, and a centrifugal force pulls in the opposite direction on the opposite side of the earth. In this case, the centrifugal force balances the sun's gravitational pull, keeping the earth in its orbit.

There are times when the line that passes through the sun and the earth is closest to the line that passes through the moon and the earth. This produces the strongest combined force. It happens when the moon is in the same direction as the sun, during a New Moon. It happens again when the moon is in the opposite direction from the sun, at a Full Moon. In both cases, the lines between the sun and earth, and the moon and earth, lie along the same general direction. They will differ only by the amount that the moon's orbit is above or below

65

the sun in the ecliptic plane. However, since this is as close as those two lines can come together during the month, the combined force is as strong as it can get during that month.

The weakest combination of forces occurs when the two lines are at right angles to each other. That happens during the First Quarter Moon and Last Quarter Moon. You can visualize that by thinking of the sun at home plate, and the First Quarter Moon at first base. The line from the moon to the earth would be at right angles to the line from the sun to the earth. At that angle, the sun's force adds its smallest contribution to the combined force. The line from the moon to the earth is at right angles to the line from the sun to the earth again when the moon is at third base, at its Last Quarter.

This means that you would feel the strongest forces at a New Moon, decreasing to a minimum at the First Quarter, rising to a maximum again at the Full Moon, and decreasing again as the moon enters its Last Quarter. We will look at these waxing and waning forces of gravity again, after we see how the moon's phases affect the waxing and waning of the electromagnetic energies that reach the earth. But before getting to that, I want to mention how the moon's orbital tilt to the ecliptic plane affects the strength of the combined force of the sun and moon.

The moon and sun have their strongest combined pull when their lines to the earth are as close as they can get to each other. We just saw how that happens at the New Moon and Full Moon, except for the fact that the moon's orbit may be above or below the sun in the ecliptic plane. However, twice each month the moon's orbit passes through the ecliptic plane: when it passes upward through the ecliptic, and again as it passes back down through the ecliptic plane. These points are called the Ascending and Descending Nodes, respectively.

The location of the Ascending and Descending Nodes changes as the tilt of the moon's orbit regresses backward through the zodiac. Table 6 in Chapter 4 will help you find where the nodes are for any date in this century. It will help you to determine if the moon was in

66

an especially strong configuration with the sun when some especially significant event occurred.

But now, let's see how the changing phases of the moon affect the electromagnetic radiations which arrive at the earth.

Moon Phase and Radiations

. In Chapter 2 you saw how the moon's surface reflected more light from the sun as it moved from a New Moon to a Full Moon. This increasing amount of light, during the waxing phases, was followed by a decreasing amount of light during the waning phases from the Full Moon, back to the New Moon. In this chapter, you have seen how the moon's phase determines when the moon will rise. The New Moon, with its minimum light, shines with the sun during the day. The Full Moon, with its maximum light, shines on the earth only after the sun goes down. The First Quarter Moon, which rises at noon, shines on the earth all afternoon, and sets at midnight. Third Quarter Moons, which rise at midnight, shine all morning until they set at noon.

You can see from all this how important the phase of the moon is in determining how much light arrives from the moon, and when that light shines during the day. (The monthly cycle of moon signs will, however, determine the length of the moon day, from moonrise to moonset.)

Until recently, it was thought that the only radiation from the moon was the light we saw reflected from the sun. However, modern measuring instruments have detected electromagnetic radiations at infrared (heat) and at microwave (radio) frequencies. These too vary with the phase of the moon, although not in the same ways that the light frequencies vary.

Infrared energies are very weak when the moon is on the sunward half of its orbit, from Third Quarter to First Quarter. At New Moon it is at its lowest level. Then, as the moon reaches its First Quarter, the infrared energy abruptly rises rapidly to about four times its lowest value. It holds at that higher level during the

Full Moon, and then a few days after the Full Moon, it falls rapidly to its low level at the Third Quarter.

Radio energies from the moon have been measured at microwave frequencies since the late 1960s. These were found to reach their maximum values about three days after the peaks of the infrared energies. In other words, the maximum and minimum radio frequency emissions are not at the Full Moon and New Moon respectively, but three days later in each case.

In the case of these other radiations, there are reasons to believe that they arise in response to the energies from the sun rather than having their source from within the moon. Regardless of their source, these energies do arrive at the earth and they vary in some relationship to the moon's phases.

The light from the moon is partially polarized. Polarization is a measure of the intensity of light energies that lie in one plane as against in another plane. As you might guess by now, the polarization of moonlight depends on the phase of the moon. It is most polarized during the First and Third Quarter Moons (more so at the Third Quarter). It is least polarized during the New Moon. During the Full Moon it is negatively polarized. That means that the electromagnetic vibrations lie mostly in the plane that passes through the earth, sun and moon at that time.

There has been a growing awareness of the importance of polarized light as a cue in orienting the response of living systems to their environment.

Another important environmental consequence of the moon's monthly phases are the apparently related changes in the earth's electric and magnetic fields. These are not the electromagnetic radiations that I have just talked about. These are the fields that arise from the earth's core and from the conditions in the atmosphere and ionosphere. The close correlations between changes in these fields and the changing phases of the moon suggest that they may be caused in part by tidal forces on the earth's core and its atmosphere.

And there are still other ways that the phases of the moon may be implicated in our constantly changing environment. One such way may be the effect it has on an

68

ocean of energies that flow down to us from the solar wind. That wind, and the moon's possible effects on it, is worth a closer look.

The Solar Wind

Everyone has been taught that space is a vacuum. In fact, we were taught that it is a perfect vacuum. Not so. The probes of the recent space programs have brought back the news that we live in the sun's atmosphere. Space is filled with particles of matter that stream out from the sun in all directions. There is a high-speed solar wind that carries energies from the sun to the earth in the form of highly charged particles structured into patterns that retain images of the sun's changing magnetic fields.

We are protected from the direct blast of the solar wind by the earth's magnetic fields, arranged into a shield called the magnetosphere. As the solar wind blows around the earth, the magnetosphere causes the earth to take on the appearance of a revolving comet, with its rounded nose toward the sun, and its long tail stretching out into space away from the sun. The nose is always toward the sun and the tail is always away from it. The New Moon is therefore always in the upstream part of the wind, and the Full Moon is always in its tail.

The solar wind that passes to the right side of the earth (looking at it from the sun) is on the dusk side of the earth. That's where the moon can be found during its First Quarter. The wind that passes to the left, on the dawn side of the earth, will be under a Third Quarter Moon. You can visualize all this if you imagine yourself as the sun at home plate, blowing a wind to the right and left of the earth, at the pitcher's mound. The first Quarter Moon is at first base, and the Third Quarter Moon is at third base, to the right and left of the mound, respectively. The right side of the earth is the dusk side because as it rotates in its counterclockwise direction, it will turn away from the sun into the darkness. The left side of the earth has just turned from darkness toward the sun, for the dawn.

The reason I mention the position of the moon's phases in the solar wind is that an exchange of energies

69

from the wind to the earth may be affected by those moon phases. For those of you who are interested in the technical aspects of this energy exchange, here is a brief summary.

Ionospheric electric fields and currents are influenced by the fields and currents generated in the magnetosphere by the passing solar wind. The extent of that influence depends on the relationship between the interplanetary magnetic field from the sun and the earth's magnetic field on the sunward side of the wind. The New Moon, on that sunward side, may have an influence on the polarity of the interplanetary magnetic field which in turn determines how it is aligned with the earth's field for a maximum energy transfer.

On the tail side of the wind, there are currents that are set up by the large-scale dawn-to-dusk electric fields in the magnetosphere. These currents are separated by a neutral plane that lies along the ecliptic plane. Local collapses in that tail current, which may be triggered by the passage of a Full Moon in the tail, divert tail currents into the ionosphere. At the same time, streams of particles can then flow through a "cleft" in the magnetic shield in the Northern Hemisphere. These streams charge up our weather systems and become visible as auroral discharges.

This exchange of energy between the magnetosphere and the ionosphere may also be strongly affected by the atmospheric tides which would reach maximum heights at dusk and dawn, during the First Quarter and Last Quarter Moons, respectively.

Perhaps I have tried to summarize too much, too briefly. This is no place to discuss the interactions of the solar wind with our environment. The controversy is still too open to claim specific mechanisms by which the phases of the moon may play a role in those interactions.

All I wanted you to recognize was that the solar wind is a newly discovered link between invisible outside energies and our environment on earth, and the moon may be standing in a very sensitive position between these outside energies and our environment.

Additionally, there are differences in the energies

70

found in the solar wind, depending on irregularly changing solar activity such as sudden flares. There are also regular changes that follow the sunspot cycle of 11 and 22 years. As these vary, they provide a changing blanket of protection from more distant cosmic energies that strike the earth. The greater the energy in the solar wind, the greater the protection it provides from the winds of other stars.

Also, the energies brought to us by the solar wind depend on the latitude of the sun from which they emerge. These may differ in polarity, strength and frequency. Winds from the sun's Northern Hemisphere differ from those from the sun's Southern Hemisphere. The moon will encounter these winds at different times, depending on whether the moon is above or below the ecliptic plane, because the sun's axis is tilted from the ecliptic plane. At certain times of the year energies from the sun's Northern Hemisphere appear above the ecliptic plane, while six months later they appear below the ecliptic plane. The moon's interaction with those energies depends on the moon's sign, which tells you whether it is above or below the ecliptic plane. That is, if you know what year it is in the Metonic cycle.

As if this weren't enough to consider, the sun also rotates on its axis once every 27 days or so (a few days more, or less, depending on the latitude of the sun that you are looking at). During that time, the solar wind changes its magnetic polarity about four times. That means that each week we see a reversal of the magnetic polarity of the solar wind. It is sometimes difficult to decide if a weekly change in the environment may be caused by these changes, or by the weekly changes in the phase of the moon. Or by both.

Let's go back now and review how our environment is influenced by the moon.

The Moon's Influence by Quadrants and Seasons

We have just seen how the moon's changing positions, as shown by its phases and signs, bring about a waxing and waning of the gravitational forces and electromagnetic energies that affect your environment. You

71

can tell when they are waxing and waning just by knowing the moon's phase and sign.

As the moon moves through its monthly phases, you can think of it as passing through each of its four quarters, or *quadrants,* as follows:

Quadrant I   —New Moon to First Quarter
Quadrant II   —First Quarter to Full Moon
Quadrant III   —Full Moon to Last Quarter
Quadrant IV   —Last Quarter to New Moon

An easy way to visualize how the forces and energies wax and wane in each of these quadrants, can be seen in Figure 3–1.

Notice that there are four squares in the figure. Each square represents the waxing and waning of a different element of the environment. Gravity, light, polarization and the infrared (heat) and microwave (radio) energies. The major moon phases are placed at the four corners of each square. Moon phases between the New Moon and First Quarter lie in the first quadrant, along side I of the square. The moon phases in the second quarter of the monthly cycle of phases lie in the second quadrant, along side II of the square. And so on, around the other sides of the square.

The changing widths (and shadings) of the sides of the squares represent the waxing and waning of the forces or energies represented by that square. For example, notice in the upper left square, the waning of the gravitational force from the New Moon to the First Quarter, shown by the narrowing width of that side, as the moon moves through the first quadrant. Waning sides are shown as shaded areas to help further identify the changes through each quadrant.

Notice also, in the square for light energy, that the brightness waxes from the New Moon to the Full Moon, as shown by the steadily increasing width of the sides of quadrants I and II.

You can use this figure to determine, for any phase of the moon, how the forces and energies are changing at that time. For example, if the moon's phase at your time of birth lies in quadrant III, you know that

72

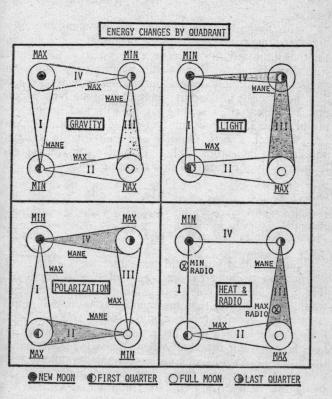

Fig. 3-1 Energy Changes by Quadrant

at the time of your birth the gravitational force, moon brightness and infrared energies were waning, while the polarization of the moonlight was waxing. When you compare those "natal" conditions with the conditions at other times of special interest, you can determine which of these energy changes may be significant in affecting your behavior.

This figure also shows you how living things which can sense the waxing and waning of gravity and light can use that information to determine the phase of the moon. For example, you can see that a waning gravity accompanied by a waxing moonlight-brightness, will tell you that the moon is in the first quadrant between New Moon and First Quarter. A waxing gravity with that same waxing brightness tells you that you are in the second quadrant, between a First Quarter and Full Moon. Perhaps you can see that more easily if I transfer some of the information from Figure 3–1 into the table below.

Quadrant	I	II	III	IV
Gravity	Wane	Wax	Wane	Wax
Moon Brightness	Wax	Wax	Wane	Wane

Suppose that you could sense that the gravity force was getting stronger over a period of several days, and that the moonlight was getting dimmer. What quadrant would that tell you that the moon was in at that time? As you look for that combination in the table you will find that the moon would be in quadrant IV, between the Last Quarter and the New Moon. If, on the other hand, the gravity force was waning for several days along with a waning moon brightness, you would know that the moon was between a Full Moon and a Last Quarter, in quadrant III.

By now it shouldn't surprise you that this same technique of measuring the changes in gravity and light can also tell you the moon sign. In this case, you would have to measure the daily change in gravity (the daily inequality) and the length of the moon day compared with the moon night. That last factor is called the light-to-

74

dark ratio (L:D). It is a factor that is known to be measured by plants and animals to help them prepare for the changes of the seasons.

Let me show you how you can tell the moon's sign from these daily changes in the daily inequality and the L:D ratio. Figure 3–2, Energy Changes by Seasons, is similar to Figure 3–1, showing energy changes by quadrant. In this case the corners of the square represent the moon signs which start each of the four seasons. Again, the increasing and decreasing widths and shadings represent the waxing and waning of the forces and energies represented by each square.

The upper left square represents the gravity forces which increase as the moon comes closer to your latitude as it moves from its position below the equator in Capricorn to above the equator in Cancer (that is, if you are above the 30th parallel of latitude, as you would be in the United States).

The upper right square represents the daily inequality, which is the difference in gravitational force between moon noon and moon midnight. You recall that this diurnal variation is greatest when the moon is in Capricorn and again when it enters Cancer. The square below that shows the variation of the gravitational force from moonrise to moon noon, and between moonset and moon midnight. Since this variation between high tide and low tide occurs twice a day, it is called the semi-diurnal variation. Notice that it waxes and wanes in an opposite way from the diurnal variation.

The lower left square represents the waxing and waning of the length of the moon day. You recall that moon days are shorter in the winter signs and longer in the summer signs. Therefore, the moon day will wax from Capricorn to Cancer. At Aries, it will be a moon equinox, with the moon days as long as the moon nights. From Cancer to Capricorn the moon days will wane, with another equinox at Libra.

If you can measure these daily differences in the force of gravity and the length of moon days and moon nights, you can tell where the moon is along the zodiac—which would tell you the moon season at that time. Let

75

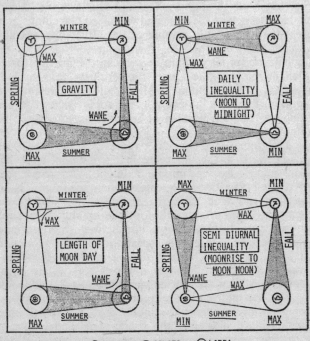

ENERGY CHANGES BY SEASONS

CAPRICORN   ARIES   CANCER   LIBRA

Fig. 3–2 Energy Changes by Seasons

76

me show you that with a table similar to the one we just used for finding the moon's phase from "measuring" the gravity and moonlight over several days.

Moon Season	Winter	Spring	Summer	Fall
Daily Inequality	Wane	Wax	Wane	Wax
Length of Moon Day	Wax	Wax	Wane	Wane

Suppose that you could sense that the daily inequality was getting smaller each day, while the length of the moon day was increasing. Where would the moon be in its season along the zodiac? If you look at the table above you can see that a waning daily inequality and a waxing moon day occur during the moon winter, between Capricorn and Aries. However, if the difference between the gravity at moon noon and moon midnight were waning, and the moon day was getting shorter, you would know that it was moon summer, and the moon was between Cancer and Libra.

Such knowledge of the status of the moon seasons must be an obvious advantage to plant and animal life in their evolutionary struggle for survival. It is no wonder then that laboratory experiments have shown how plant and animal behavior can be triggered and controlled by changes in the durations of light cycles and gravitational forces. Although there is little information on the mechanisms involved in such responses, there is little question that animals and plants sense and respond to these basic forces in the environment. Let's take a look at some of those responses.

Sensing and Responding to the Environment

The late Rachel L. Carson, in her best-seller *The Sea Around Us,* reported on the strange behavior of the palolo worm which lives under the sea near Samoa, in the South Pacific. Twice each year these worms break in two, so that their reproductive halves can float to the surface to mingle with others in a massive spawning. This happens in October and November at dawn of the day before the moon reaches its Last Quarter, and again the next day.

How do these worms know when to begin this annual act of reproduction? Let's see what they could learn from the measurement of gravity forces.

The sun would be in Scorpio and Sagittarius from October through November. These are the signs of spring in the Southern Hemisphere. They would correspond with the April and May signs of Taurus and Gemini in the Northern Hemisphere. As the sun moves from Scorpio to Sagittarius it passes over the latitude of Samoa, producing its strongest gravitational pull over that area.

But why a Third Quarter moon, and why at dawn?

When the sun is over Samoa, the Third Quarter Moon would be as far north of the equator as the sun is south of it. The earth-moon line would then line up with the earth-sun line with respect to the earth's equator, producing a maximum combination of their gravitational forces. The palolo worm would know that the moon is in this position if it noticed that the moon's pull was at maximum at dawn. That's because a Third Quarter Moon rises at midnight and reaches moon noon six hours later, at dawn. Moon noon produces a maximum pull.

If backup cues were needed, perhaps they might come from the maximum polarization of the moonlight which occurs during a Third Quarter Moon. Such polarization might affect the ability of moonlight to penetrate to the shallow sea floor where the palolo worm lives with its better half until it is "time."

This speculation about the palolo worm's ability to know when its time has come is based on an assumption of its ability to sense when the moon is overhead. But is there any evidence that animals have such a sense? Yes! Thanks to the now classic experiments of Dr. Frank A. Brown, Jr., Morrison Professor of Biological Sciences at Northwestern University, Evanston, Illinois. He showed that oysters open their valves to feed whenever the moon passes overhead. That would correspond with a local high tide if the oysters were at a coastline.

Dr. Brown demonstrated this by transporting oysters from their home on an eastern seashore, to his laboratory at Evanston, Illinois. At first the oysters' feeding cycle remained in step with the tide cycles of the East Coast. However, within two weeks they changed over to a feeding cycle that would have corresponded with a high-tide cycle at a coastline, if one existed, at Evanston, Illinois.

The grunion (small, slender food fish) not only know when the moon is overhead but can keep track of the moon's changing position for several days. It has to be able to do that to know when the New Moon and Full Moon will arrive with the two highest tides of the month. The grunion ride these highest tides to their crest to deposit their eggs in the sand. The eggs are then safe from the successively lower tides. Two weeks later, the highest tide arrives to help release the fishlets from their eggs and to wash them out to sea. This behavior suggests that the grunion can measure the waxing and waning energies which then act as the signals of an upcoming New Moon or Full Moon.

Increasingly, more researchers are discovering the links between lunar cycles and animal behavior. Fiddler crabs forage on the beaches in time with moonrise and moonset. Rats in isolation change their activity patterns in accordance with moonrise and moonsets they never see. But they don't have to see them, since the forces of gravity, which cannot be shielded, tell them when the forces are at their lowest, as they would be at moonrise and moonset.

The sensitivity of animals to changing patterns of light has been studied for many years. Seasonal changes in the the ratio of light to darkness are now recognized as the regulators of seasonably appropriate behavior. Sexual activities, preparation for hibernation, food gathering and other complex behaviors are triggered or controlled by hormonal secretions that are in turn regulated by the changes in the light-to-dark cycles associated with each season.

Perhaps less directly, but just as effectively, the moon affects us by its indirect effect on the weather. The link between the moon and our weather has become less a matter of folklore and more a matter of record. Extensive studies now show that thunderstorms, which recharge our atmosphere, occur most often after a New

Moon and a Full Moon. You might want to check that for yourself by keeping track of moon phases and thunderstorms. But you should keep in mind that the studies considered thunderstorms on a worldwide basis, and your local weather may have its own patterns.

Other studies show that there are more days of rain, and more rain on those days, when the moon is furthest from the equator. These are the days which the farmer's almanacs describe as "moon rides high," or "moon rides low." You can confirm this yourself by keeping track of the moon signs on rainy days. You should find that there are more rainy days when the moon is near the solstice signs of Cancer and Capricorn, and less rain during the equinox signs of Aries and Libra. When the moon is in the equinox signs the farmer's almanacs say that the "moon is on the equator."

The growing acceptance of the moon's role in our weather stems in part from a growing understanding of the interaction between lunar tides and daily sun (heat) tides in our atmosphere. Evidence also continues to accumulate for lunar periodicities in the earth's magnetic fields, electric fields, ionization levels and other energies which affect, or are affected by, our weather systems.

These moon-related weather fields are now believed to have physiological and psychological effects to the extent that they influence reaction times and mood-modifying body chemistry. Increasing amounts of ionization in the air, which follows a lunar cycle, have been traced to their effects on response times thought to be responsible for increasing accident rates. Serotonin, a mood-modifying body chemical, responds to increasing ionization levels, causing irritability episodes which disappear as those levels return to normal. The role of ionization in our atmosphere is under renewed study. Perhaps we will soon have a pI index, showing the percentage of ionization in the air we breathe, just as we now have a pH index showing the percentage of ionization of the liquids we use. In both cases we would be concerned with assuring a proper ratio of positive and negative charges in our gaseous and liquid environment, both of which may be responsive to the changing positions of the moon.

This common denominator of a single "source" of

the physical and psychological patterns of behavior may not be as remote as it first seems. Dr. Frank Brown found that the metabolism of cells, all kinds of cells, follows lunar cycles. He found daily, weekly, fortnightly, monthly and longer-term cycles of metabolic activity which were linked to the moon, regardless of the type of cells under consideration.

And these cellular-level behaviors may have an even more fundamental common lunar basis. They all depend on the presence of water. Professor Giorgio Piccardi and others have found that the properties of water change with the lunar cycle. The structure of water consists of pyramids of hydrogen and oxygen atoms bonded by fragile links that respond to changing electric and magnetic fields of the size that are known to vary with lunar passages. The chemical consequences of these monthly variations in the properties of water may be responsible for some part of the physical and psychological cycles which mysteriously follow those same lunar passages.

Environmental Imprinting

One of the questions that often comes up is, If the moon affects us, why doesn't it affect all of us the same way at the same time? Good question! Why are some people seemingly disturbed by the Full Moon, while others are not? Why do some people seem more at ease during a waning moon, while others feel better during a waxing moon?

No one really knows for sure.

Some say that the moon's energies have different effects on you depending on where your energies are at the time. I'm sure that's part of it. But I believe that it has more to do with our environmental imprinting at the time of our birth.

The concept of imprinting comes from biology. Certain conditions, which appear at critical moments in the development of the individual, are permanently stored or imprinted into the memory of the individual. That memory, stored into the cells of the body, then serves as a reference for regulating future behavior. For example, a

81

newly hatched duckling is programmed to follow the first thing that it sees. Normally that would be its mother. However, if it sees a person instead of its mother, that person becomes imprinted on the duckling as its "mother."

I believe that in a similar way we are imprinted with the environmental conditions that prevailed at the time of our birth. Those natal conditions are "remembered" by their patterns of gravity and light energies, stored in the structure and chemistry of our body cells. Those patterns represent the "natal season of our birth."

Early in our evolution we must have been programmed to be born at the most favorable season for survival (much as the palolo worm is still programmed to be born at its best season, as determined by the positions of the sun and moon). Once born, there are seasons to grow and go forth, to gather food, to reproduce, to hide from the elements, and even to die.

Nature has provided us with a repertoire of seasonally appropriate behaviors to be implemented during each of these seasons, following from that season of birth. That could be done by triggering or controlling our responses on the basis of a comparison between the current conditions and our imprinted natal conditions. Or, by counting the number of seasons since the natal season. In either case, the resulting behavior patterns would be seasonally appropriate only if the imprinted natal conditions represented the favored season of birth. Those born "in season" would find their activities waxing and waning in harmony with the energy patterns of the successive seasons of their lives.

However, if by chance you are born "out of season," the conditions of your natal season are still imprinted on you as though it were the proper season of birth. The programmed behavior in response to that wrong imprinting would then be out of phase with the subsequent seasons. Your responses would follow the wrong natal season just as the duckling follows the wrong mother. Fortunately, we have become so adaptable that we can follow the wrong seasonal imprinting without fatal consequences. A more serious problem today is that, even with correct seasonal imprinting, our programmed responses may be wrong for the man-made environment in which we live.

The point of all this is simple. If you were born at a season which evolution has favored for the survival of our species, then your responses will be in harmony with the changing seasons. That includes moon seasons as well as sun seasons. The relationship between those two seasons is shown by the phase of the moon. If certain phases of the moon are troublesome for you, it signifies that certain combinations of the sun and moon seasons are more difficult for you than others. That would depend on the season of your birth.

I will show you, in the next chapter, how to find the moon phases, moon signs and sun signs so that you can compare your season of birth with the seasons in which things go well for you and those that bring you difficulties.

But before getting into that, let me make an interesting observation about this matter of imprinting. I have noticed that our biorhythms, those internal tides of biological energies, have relationships between them which are the same as relationships between several of the moon's periodic motions. It may very well be that biorhythms, beginning as they do on the day of our birth, are the clocks which help keep us in step with the changing environmental conditions related to the changing moon positions. Those clocks, starting as they would from the imprinted natal conditions, are probably kept accurate by periodic sensing of the forces and fields associated with specific moon positions.

The question of the role of biorhythms as internal synchronizers to external environmental periodicities is an involved one. Although biorhythm cycles do not have the same periods as the moon-motion cycles, there are periodicities in the crossings and merges of certain pairs of biorhythms which are the same as some periodicities between pairs of moon cycles.

Summary

The moon gets to you by affecting your environment, directly and indirectly. Its changing positions affect the forces of gravity and electromagnetic energies in

83

daily, weekly, monthly and yearly cycles. The timing and duration of these cycles depend on the positions of the sun and moon with respect to each other, and with respect to the earth's equator. Those positions are shown by the moon's phases, and by the sun signs and moon signs which identify the sun seasons and moon seasons.

The changing phases and signs determine how the forces of gravity and light wax and wane. Daily "measures" of such energies reveal the moon's position to animals which may then regulate their behavior to take advantage of upcoming conditions in their environment.

Your responses to changing moon positions may be regulated by your "measures" of the environment which are then compared with your imprinted natal conditions. That comparison leads to behavior that may be favorable or difficult for you, depending on your natal conditions.

You can investigate these responses by comparing your natal moon positions with the moon positions on favorable or difficult days, to find your better phases and signs.

Another Postscript

In a subject as complex as this, it is necessary to pass over important points along the way to avoid unnecessary confusion. Two such points come to mind. First, those of you who know something about the tides know that high tides don't necessarily occur at moon noon or moon midnight. The tides can vary considerably in time and height along the same shoreline. That's because other forces are at work besides the gravitational pull of the sun and moon.

Ocean floors and river beds have changing depths and slopes, and other obstacles to the flow of the waters. Also, many bodies of water lie in giant basins in which the waters rock back and forth as though in a large pan. As the water rocks back and forth in its basin, it will rise higher at the ends of the basin than at its center. And the period of the oscillation, driven by the moon, will depend as much on the dimensions of the basin as it does on the time of the moon's passages. You would need more than a Daily Moon Chart (Fig. 4–2) to determine the height and timing of the tides on the earth.

The second point is this. Although the moon's pull is strongest at moon noon and moon midnight, it's not the strongest pull that you feel during the day. That's because the greatest pull depends on how the moon's pull combines with the sun's pull. And that depends on the phase of the moon when the moon is in the first and third quadrants, the combined pull being strongest before the moon noon or moon midnight. When the moon is in the second and fourth quadrants, the combined pull is strongest after the moon noon or moon midnight.

However, in either case, the influence of the moon's pull is still strongest during moon noon and moon midnight.

One final comment. These tidal forces that we have been looking at are really composed of a vertical and horizontal component. We have been focusing our attention on the vertical components, which are maximum away from the earth at the moon's zenith and nadir, and maximum into the earth at moonrise and moonset. However, the horizontal components of these tidal forces also change from zero values at the noons, midnights, moonrises and moonsets to become strongest at the intermediate times between those peaks of the vertical forces. Those horizontal components also vary with latitude, and can provide a rich source for the study of gravitational effects of the moon on animal behavior on earth.

4
Where Is the
Moon Today?

Introduction

This is the chapter that I have been telling you all about. It's the one in which I have collected all the tables and charts that will help you find out where the moon is at any time. There are tables for finding the moon's phases and others for finding the moon's signs. There are charts for finding where the moon is during the day and others for finding where it is in its 18.6-year cycle.

Let me explain how to use this chapter. First, you will want to know where the moon was on the day you were born. That will be your "natal moon." You look up your moon phase, moon sign and the time of moon noon (if you know the hour of your birth). You also look up the tilt of the moon's orbit, which tells you the severity of the moon seasons in the year you were born. All these, taken together, give you a profile of the moon environment that was imprinted on you the day you were born.

Once you know your natal conditions, you then look up the moon conditions for dates of special interest.

These will be the dates of periods or events during which you found yourself at peak performance, or in the doldrums. And then you will compare these event moon conditions with your natal moon conditions to see how they might be related. (I'll show you how to do that in Chapter 5.)

You can also use these tables and charts to check on the relationships between your natal moon conditions and those of your companions—compatible companions, and those who always seem to be at the root of your problems. Again, you check the moon conditions for patterns that may show you when you can expect a compatible relationship and when you can expect a troubled one. I'll show you how to check that in Chapter 6.

And then, if you are a woman, or are a man interested in a special woman, I will show you how to use these tables to check on the strictly feminine functions that are influenced by the moon. That is in Chapter 7.

In each of these applications, you will need a convenient way to compare the different moon conditions under consideration. I will show you some easy-to-use plotting procedures to do that, later in this chapter.

Finally, some of you may be wondering about what your moon has to say about you astrologically. To check that out, first find the moon phase and moon sign for your birthday, using the tables in this chapter. Then, in Chapter 8, you can find a brief astrological profile based on these and other considerations.

Now, let's get on with it. We will start with the moon's phases.

How to Find The Moon's Phase

The two-part Moon Phase Table (Table 3) is used for finding the phase of the moon for any date in the 1800s or 1900s. The table is based on a 2400-year-old discovery by Meton, a Greek astronomer. Meton noticed that the same phases of the moon would appear on the same days of the year, every nineteen years. He must have been a patient observer!

Meton's discovery lets you predict the moon's phase for any month, once you know the phases for each

87

MOON PHASE TABLE (PART I) - FOR YEAR AND MONTH

PART I - FIND THE KEY LETTER AT THE INTERSECTION OF THE YEAR (ROW) AND THE MONTH (COLUMN) FOR THE DATE OF INTEREST.

PART II - FIND THE DAY OF THE MONTH ON THAT KEY LETTER ROW, THE NUMBER OF THAT DAY-COLUMN IS THE MOON (PHASE) AGE IN DAYS.

YEAR OF INTEREST					JAN	FEB	MAR	APR	MAY	JUN	JUL	AUG	SEP	OCT	NOV	DEC
1900	1919	1938	1957	1976	P	N	O	N	M	L	K	J	H	H	F	F
1901	1920	1939	1958	1977	E	C	D	C	B	A	DD	CC	AA	AA	Y	Y
1902	1921	1940	1959	1978	X	V	V	V	U	T	S	P	P	P	N	N
1903	1922	1941	1960	1979	M	K	L	K	J	I	H	E	E	E	C	C
1904	1923	1942	1961	1980	B	DD	A	DD	CC	BB	AA	X	X	X	V	V
1905	1924	1943	1962	1981	U	S	T	S	R	Q	P	M	M	M	K	K
1906	1925	1944	1963	1982	J	H	I	H	G	F	E	D	B	B	DD	DD
1907	1926	1945	1964	1983	CC	AA	BB	AA	Z	Y	X	U	U	U	S	S
1908	1927	1946	1965	1984	R	P	Q	P	O	N	M	L	J	J	H	H
1909	1928	1947	1966	1985	G	E	F	E	D	C	B	A	CC	CC	AA	AA
1910	1929	1948	1967	1986	Z	X	Y	X	W	V	U	T	R	R	P	P
1911	1930	1949	1968	1987	O	M	N	M	L	K	J	I	G	G	E	E
1912	1931	1950	1969	1988	D	B	C	B	A	DD	CC	BB	Z	Z	X	X
1913	1932	1951	1970	1989	W	U	V	U	T	S	Q	Q	O	O	M	M
1914	1933	1952	1971	1990	L	J	K	J	I	H	G	F	D	D	B	B
1915	1934	1953	1972	1991	A	CC	DD	CC	BB	AA	Z	Y	W	W	U	U
1916	1935	1954	1973	1992	T	R	S	R	Q	P	O	N	L	L	J	J
1917	1936	1955	1974	1993	I	G	H	G	F	E	D	C	A	A	CC	CC
1918	1937	1956	1975	1994	BB	Z	AA	Z	Y	X	W	V	T	T	R	R

MOON PHASE TABLE (PART II) - FOR DAY OF MONTH

NEW MOON — FIRST QUARTER — FULL MOON — LAST QUARTER

ROW NUMBERS ARE DAYS OF MONTH (FOR DAY-31, USE "1"). LARGER NUMBERS ARE MOON'S AGES.

ROW-LETTER FROM PART I OF MOON PHASE TABLE

Table 3   Moon Phase Table

89

month in any nineteen-year sequence. The Moon Phase Table tells you just that. Part I of the table gives you the key to the moon's phases for any month of any year. Part II then uses that key to give you the phase for any day in that month. You will see how that works by following me through some examples.

Elvis Presley was born on January 8, 1935. To find the phase of the moon on the day he was born, we begin with the Moon Phase Table (Part I)—for Year and Month. Please take a look at it now. Notice the columns of numbers under the heading "Year of Interest," and the columns of letters under the heading "Month of Interest." Each of the columns of numbers represents a nineteen-year sequence of Meton's cycle.

Start by looking down the columns of numbers until you find your year of interest. In this case we are looking for the year 1935. You will find it near the bottom of the second column (third from the bottom).

Now move your finger across the 1935 row until you get to the letter column representing your month of interest. In this case it's the first column, January. The months are shown across the top of the columns. You should have found the letter "T" at the intersection of the 1935 row and the January column. That letter is your key to Part II of the Moon Phase Table. Please look at that part now.

Notice the column of letters on both sides of the table. These are the key letters you get from Part I. The key letter puts you in the proper row for finding the moon phase for any day in the month and year represented by that key letter.

The rows of numbers across the table are the days of the month, in your month of interest. In our case, we are interested in January 8. Move your finger across row T (for January 1935) until you find the number 8. (The eighth of the month in row T happens to be near the beginning of that row, but the day of the month can be anywhere along the row, depending on what row it is.)

Once you find the day of the month in a row, look up or down that column to the larger-sized numbers that are at the top and bottom of the table. In our case, the

90

larger number in our column is 3. These larger numbers represent the phase of the moon for that day, expressed in terms of the moon's age, in days. You recall that the moon's age begins at 0 days with the New Moon. A moon age of 3 means that it is 3 days after a New Moon. That tells us that Elvis Presley was born 3 days after a New Moon. It was therefore a Waxing Crescent Moon.

You may have already noticed that the rows of dates in Part II do not include the thirty-first of the month. When you have to look up the moon's phase for the thirty-first of any month, use the column for the first of that month.

Although the Moon Phase Table covers the years from 1900 to 1994, you can use it for any year in the 1800s as well as for the 1900s. You simply add 19 years to the 1800 date until the date falls into the 1900s. For instance, $1865 + 19 = 1884$; $1884 + 19 = 1903$. Use that date to find the moon's phase for the month and day of interest. However, once you find it, you must add one day to the moon's age to account for the change of the century. Let me show you how that works.

Pope Paul VI was born on September 26, 1897. What was the phase of the moon on his birthday? If you add 19 years to 1897, you get 1916. Using Part I of the Moon Phase Table you find that the key letter for September 1916 is "L." Then, in Part II, in row L, the twenty-sixth of the month is in the last column. The moon's age, shown at the top of that column, is 29 days. That is the last day of a moon cycle. (A moon age of 30 days is the same as a moon age of 0 days.) When you add one day to day 29 to account for the change of century, you move to the beginning of the next cycle, to a moon age of 0 days.

So, Pope Paul VI was born under a New Moon.

You could use this process to reach back into the 1700s, but no further back than 1753—that's when a major calendar revision was adopted by England and its colonies.

Now it's time for you to try the Moon Phase Table. See if you can find the moon's phase on June 22, 1954. That was the date that Freddie Prinze was born. He was Chico, in the TV series, *Chico and the Man.*

91

Here is all you have to do.

1. Find the key letter for the *month* and *year* of interest from Part I of the Moon Phase Table.
2. Find the row in Part II of the table that corresponds with that key letter.
3. Find the *day* of the month of interest along that row. If the day is the thirty-first, use the first.
4. Find the *moon's age,* in days, at the top or bottom of the column that contains your day of the month.

In your example you should have found the key letter for June 1954 to be "P." Then, in row P in Part II you should have found that the twenty-second of the month is in the column headed by a large 21. You can see from the symbols across the top that a moon age of 21 days represents a moon phase that is one day before the Last Quarter Moon.

Let's try one more. This time one that will give you experience with finding a moon phase in the 1800s. Franklin Delano Roosevelt was born on January 30, 1882. What was the moon's phase at the time he was born? Try it.

You should have found a moon age of 11 days. That would be halfway between a First Quarter and a Full Moon. A Waxing Gibbous Moon.

The year 1882 becomes 1901 when you add 19 years. The key letter for January 1901 is "E." The thirtieth of the month in row E, in Part II, is in the column for a moon age of 10 days. Remember to add one day for the change of century, and you end up with 11 days for the moon's age.

Now find the moon's phase for the day you were born. Move on then to see how you can find the moon's signs.

How to Find Moon Signs—the Decan Table

The moon sign is the sign of the zodiac in which the moon can be found on any date. During a New Moon the moon is in the same sign of the zodiac as the sun. During a First Quarter Moon the moon is one-quarter of

92

the way around the zodiac, ahead of the sun. Since one-quarter of the twelve-sign zodiac is three signs, the First Quarter Moon is always three signs of the zodiac ahead of the sun sign at that time.

A Full Moon is on the opposite side of the zodiac from the sun. A Last Quarter Moon (Third Quarter) is three-quarters of the zodiac ahead of the sun, or one-quarter of the zodiac behind it. The moon's sign during a Last Quarter Moon is therefore always three signs behind the sun sign at that time. From this you can see that if you know the sun's sign, the moon's phase then can help you find the moon's sign. Table 4, the Decan Moon Sign Table, does that for you.

The column of dates on the left side of the table represents increments of about 10 days each, called decans. There are thirty-six decans in a year, three for each sign of the zodiac. The signs of the zodiac corresponding with each decan are shown by their symbols in the table just after their dates. These are the signs in which the sun can be found on those decan dates; they are the sun signs during those dates. If you are not familiar with the symbols for the signs of the zodiac, you can check them against Table 1 in Chapter 2.

The large-sized numbers across the top of this table also represent the moon's phase, expressed in days of the moon's age. These are the same numbers you get from Part II of the Moon Phase Table (Table 3).

The Decan Moon Sign Table is designed so that the intersection of the date row and the moon age column shows you the number of the decan in which the moon can be found on that date. The moon's sign that corresponds with that decan number can be found in front of the decan numbers shown in the first column of the table.

Let me show you how to use the Decan Moon Sign Table. What was Elvis Presley's moon sign? That would be the moon's sign on the day he was born, January 8, 1935. You already found that the moon's age was 3 days on that date. The next step then is to look at the Decan Moon Sign Table for the intersection of that moon age and the date January 8.

You begin by looking for the row of dates that in-

93

DECAN MOON SIGN TABLE

MOON AGE (DAYS)	0	1	2	3	4	5	6	7	8	9	10	11	12	13	14	15	16	17	18	19	20	21	22	23	24	25	26	27	28	29
DATE OF INTEREST																														
JAN 1-10																														
JAN 11-20																														
JAN 21-30																														
JAN 31-FEB 9																														
FEB 10-19																														
FEB 20-MAR 1																														
MAR 2-11																														
MAR 12-21																														
MAR 22-31																														
APR 1-10																														
APR 11-20																														
APR 21-30																														
MAY 1-11																														
MAY 12-21																														
MAY 22-JUN 1																														
JUN 2-11																														
JUN 12-21																														
JUN 22-JUL 2																														
JUL 3-12																														
JUL 13-23																														
JUL 24-AUG 2																														
AUG 3-13																														
AUG 14-23																														
AUG 24-SEP 3																														
SEP 4-13																														
SEP 14-23																														
SEP 24-OCT 3																														
OCT 4-13																														
OCT 14-23																														
OCT 24-NOV 3																														
NOV 4-12																														
NOV 13-22																														
NOV 23-DEC 2																														
DEC 3-12																														
DEC 13-22																														
DEC 23-31																														

Table 4   Decan Moon Sign Table

94

cludes January 8. In this case you would find it in the top row, the one for January 1–10. Run your finger across that row until you come to the moon age column identified by the large 3 at the top of the table.

The number you find at the intersection of that date row and moon age column is the number of the decan in which you would find the moon on January 8, 1935. In this case, the moon would be in decan 33. If you now check the signs in front of the first column of decan numbers, you will find that decan 33 corresponds with the third decan of Aquarius. Aquarius runs from decan 31 to 33. Again, if you need help in recognizing the symbols for the signs of the zodiac, they are in Chapter 2, Table 1.

Let me point out something about the decan numbers in that first column. That column is for a moon age of 0 days. That means that it is for the New Moon. You remember that the New Moon is in the same sign of the zodiac as the sun. Therefore, the decan numbers for a New Moon must also be the decan numbers for the sun's position, on those same dates. In other words, the numbers in the first column, for moon age 0 days, are also the decan numbers for the sun signs on the dates in each row.

The reason I mention this is because we will want to use the sun sign decan numbers later, along with the moon sign decan numbers. You can get both from Table 4. For example, you can see that Elvis Presley's sun sign, in the decan row for January 8, is in decan 29. That is the second decan of Capricorn. Elvis, then, had a Capricorn sun and an Aquarius moon. Astrologically that means that he had the courage to blaze new trails, the need for independence, and problems with feelings of insecurity.

At this point, you've probably looked up your own moon sign. If you're curious about its astrological significance you can look it up in Chapter 8.

How to Find Moon Signs—the Zodiac Chart

Finding the moon signs and sun signs in terms of the number of decans makes it convenient to analyze the relationships between them. Decan numbers can be plotted in different ways to reveal interesting relationships and patterns. But once you know what you might be look-

95

ing for, you may want a more direct reading for moon signs and sun signs. The Zodiac Moon Sign Chart (Fig. 4–1) was designed to help you do just that. Please take a look at it.

Notice that the column on the left side of the chart provides you with the same listing of decan dates that you had with the Decan Moon Sign Table. Also, the numbers across the top and bottom of the chart still represent the number of days of the moon's age. However, there are no decan numbers on this chart. Instead, there are diagonal bands across the chart, each one representing a different sign of the zodiac.

This chart is used in the same way that you used the Decan Moon Sign Table. The moon's sign for any date and moon age is shown at the intersection of the date row and the moon age column. For example, notice how the 3-day moon age column and the January 8 date row for Elvis Presley's birthday lead you to an intersection in the shaded area identified as Aquarius. You may remember that the Decan Moon Sign Table also showed the moon sign as Aquarius.

The Zodiac Moon Sign Chart gives you the same information as the table, except that it gives it to you directly in terms of the zodiac symbol instead of a decan number. It also shows you something about moon signs which can't be seen as easily from the table. The moon moves around the zodiac so fast that it goes from one sign to the next in about 2½ days. The places at which the moon signs change are called cusps. The moon passes through a cusp every 2½ days. On each of those cusp days there are two moon signs. The moon is in one sign during the first part of the day, and in the next sign during the second part of the day.

When you use the Decan Moon Sign Table you should be alerted to a possible cusp day whenever the moon sign decan number is in the first or third decan of a sign. Presley's moon sign was in the third decan of Aquarius. A possible cusp day.

If you now look at the Zodiac Moon Sign Chart you will see that cusp situation more easily. Look at the intersection where you found Presley's moon sign (moon age 3 days, January 8). Notice how the diagonal bound-

96

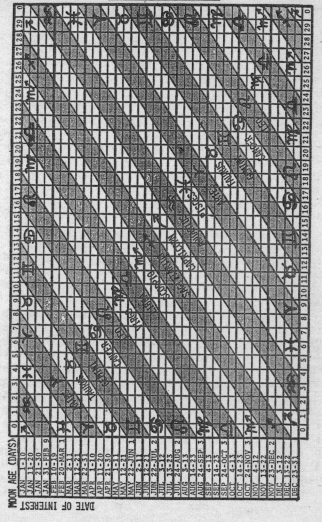

Fig. 4–1 Zodiac Moon Sign Chart

97

ary between Aquarius and Pisces passes right through that intersection. If you check with an ephemeris you will find that the moon was in Aquarius until 7 A.M. on January 8. After that it moved into Pisces, which follows the sign of Aquarius in the zodiac.

Moon sign tables and charts (even mine) are not as accurate as the more detailed listings of an ephemeris. (However, their accuracy is adequate for our purposes, and they are compact and easy to use.) That's why most sources advise you to consider the moon signs on both sides of a cusp day when you are dealing with rapidly changing moon signs to see which may be more fitting in your case.

Before moving on to the next section, be sure that you know how to use the Zodiac Moon Sign Chart. Find the moon sign for the birthdate of Freddie Prinze. His birthdate was June 22, 1954. You recall that the moon's age for that date was 21 days. Now look at the Zodiac Moon Sign Chart. First find the date row that includes June 22. Run your finger across that row until you get to the column for a moon age of 21 days. The intersection of that date row and moon age column falls clearly in the diagonal area identified as Pisces, which means that Freddie Prinze's moon sign was in Pisces. Let me show you how to find his sun sign from this chart.

Notice that the diagonal area which touches the June 22 date row at the 0 day first column is identified as Cancer. That first column represents the New Moon. Since the sun sign is the same as the moon sign on the date of a New Moon, the sun sign on June 22 is Cancer. Which means that Freddie Prinze's sun sign was Cancer and his moon sign was Pisces. One astrological source puts it this way: "If you are betrayed by your lover, you may become severely depressed. . . ." Freddie shot himself after failing at a reconciliation with his wife.

Notice that if the moon's age had been 22 days in that date row, the moon's sign might also have been in Aries. In that case you would recognize it as a cusp day and consider both signs as possible moon signs for the day.

You saw in Chapter 3 how the moon's influence varies throughout the day. You saw that its gravitational pull was weakest at moonrise and moonset and strongest at moon noon and moon midnight. When you start looking for the moon's influences in your life, you will want to know whether certain feelings rise with the moon, or reach their peaks at moon noon. Some tensions may culminate with the setting moon, or be triggered by a moonmidnight. If you want to check these out you have to know where the moon is in its daily passage between moonrise and moonset. You may remember that it all depends on the phase of the moon on the day in question.

Figure 4–2, Daily Moon Chart, will give you the times of moonrise, moon noon, moonset and moon midnight for any day. All you need to know is the phase of the moon on that day, either in terms of the moon's age in days, or the moon's shapes as shown by the eight symbols on the chart.

The moon's phases, in days of moon age, are shown across the top and bottom of the chart. The time of day is shown along the sides of the chart. Standard Time is shown on the left. Daylight Saving Time is shown on the right.

The diagonal lines and the shaded areas between them help you to see where the moon is at any time of day. The diagonal lines are identified as Moonrise, Moon Noon, Moonset, and Moon Midnight. The terms "maximum" and "minimum" on the lines refer to the strength of the gravitational pull that is experienced at that time. Shaded areas represent the moon nights that lie between moonset and moonrise lines. The unshaded areas represent the times during which there is moonlight on earth.

Now let's see how we can use this chart. Suppose that you are a woman, and that you made a note that your last menstrual cycle began at 1 P.M. on a day when the moon's age was 2 days. The question is, where was the moon at that time? Was it at moonrise, moonset, or elsewhere? Look at the Daily Moon Chart.

99

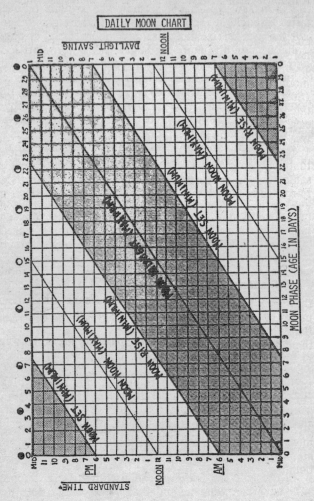

Fig. 4-2 Daily Moon Chart

100

First, locate the vertical line that corresponds with a moon age of 2 days. Run your finger up that line until you get to a horizontal line that corresponds with a time of 1 P.M. Afternoon hours are on the upper part of the chart, morning hours are on the lower part. Noon is across the middle of the chart.

You can see that the intersection of the line for a moon age of 2 days and the line representing 1 P.M. (Standard Time) falls just below the diagonal line identified as Moon Noon—Maximum. This means that in this case the woman's menstrual cycle began just as the moon was reaching its maximum gravitational pull of the day.

Once you find where the moon is during a particular time, you can use the chart to see when it will be in the same position (or an equivalent one) at some future date. For example, if this woman has a regular 27-day cycle, what time of day can she expect her next menstrual cycle to begin? If we assume that her cycle is triggered by a maximum gravitational pull, we can use the chart to find out what time that can be expected.

Adding 27 days to the moon's age of 2 days, the moon's phase at her last cycle, means that her next cycle will start when the moon's age is 29 days. If you look at the chart you will see that there is a maximum pull at moon noon, which occurs at 11 A.M. on that day. Standard Time is read from the scale on the left side of the chart. Therefore, she should expect her period to start at 11 A.M.

It could also start at 11 P.M. that same night. Notice that there is another maximum pull where the vertical moon age line for 29 days intersects the diagonal line identified as Moon Midnight. Remember, there are two times each day when the moon reaches a maximum gravitational pull and two times when it has a minimum pull (moonrise and moonset). You have to check both times when you are trying to make a prediction.

Fine-Tuning the Daily Moon Chart

In later chapters I will show you other ways to use the Daily Moon Chart to check for the moon's influence on your life. For most applications you will use the chart

101

just as it is. However, in some cases you may want to make corrections to account for the fact that moonrise and moonset times depend on the moon sign and on your latitude on the earth.

The moonrise and moonset times depend on moon sign, just as the sunrise and sunset times depend on the sun sign. During the spring and summer signs, Aries through Libra, the sun and moon rise earlier and set later. During the fall and winter signs, Libra through Aries, the sun and moon rise later and set earlier. During the solstices, in Cancer and Capricorn, the rising and setting times may be as much as an hour and a half different from the times shown on the Daily Moon Chart. The times of moon noon and moon midnight are not affected by moon sign.

The effects of latitude on the time of rising and setting times may surprise you. During spring and summer signs, Aries through Libra, the sun and the moon rise earlier and set later in the north than they do in the south. During the fall and winter signs, Libra through Aries, the sun and the moon rise later and set sooner in the north than they do in the south. The differences in the rising and setting times are, at most, about a half hour from the times shown on the Daily Moon Chart. And that happens only when the moon is in the signs of Cancer and Capricorn.

Most of the time the moonrise and moonset times that you find from the chart will be more than adequate for your purposes. However, for those of you who may want to make an occasional "fine-tuning" correction to the times shown on the Daily Moon Chart, I have provided additional tables. These are the Correction Tables for Moonrise and Moonset (Table 5). The tables give you the times to be added to or subtracted from the moonrise and moonset times found on the Daily Moon Chart. Here's how to use the tables.

Corrections for Moon Sign
1. Find the moon sign for the day of interest, using the Zodiac Moon Sign Chart (Fig. 4–1).
2. Find that moon sign on the Table of Corrections for Moon Sign Seasons, Part I.
3. Notice the number of hours to be added or sub-

102

tracted from the times found on the Daily Moon Chart.

4. If you are correcting for a *moonrise,* add or subtract that number of hours, as instructed at the *top* of the column in which you found the moon sign.

5. If you are correcting for a *moonset,* add or subtract that number of hours, as instructed at the bottom of the column in which you found the moon sign.

Notice that there are no corrections needed when the moon is in Aries or Libra, the equinox signs.

Corrections for Latitude

The Daily Moon Chart shows the correct times of moonrise and moonset for places that are not too far from the 40th parallel of latitude across the United States. That means you do not have to make corrections for places that lie near a line that passes through New York City, Chicago, Denver, Salt Lake City, or Sacramento, California. In fact, no corrections are needed until you get close to the northern or southern borders of the United States. (That would be 50 degrees latitude and 30 degrees latitude, respectively.) When you want to make corrections for those latitudes, here's all you have to do.

1. Find the moon sign for the day of interest, using the Zodiac Moon Sign Chart (Fig. 4–1).

2. Find that moon sign on the Table of Corrections for Latitudes, Part II.

3. Notice the number of minutes to be added to or subtracted from the times found on the Daily Moon Chart.

4. If you are correcting for a *moonrise,* add or subtract that number of minutes, as instructed at the *top* of the column in which you found the moon sign. (Notice that the instruction depends on whether you are *north* or *south* of the 40th parallel.)

5. If you are correcting for a *moonset,* add or subtract that number of minutes, as instructed at the *bottom* of the column in which you found the

CORRECTION TABLES FOR MOONRISE AND MOONSET

I - TABLE OF CORRECTIONS FOR MOON SIGN SEASONS

FOR MOONRISE		HOURS TO ADD
SUBTRACT	ADD	OR SUBTRACT
ARIES	LIBRA	NONE
TAURUS	SCORPIO	3/4
GEMINI	SAGITTARIUS	1 1/4
CANCER	CAPRICORN	1 1/2
LEO	AQUARIUS	1 1/4
VIRGO	PISCES	3/4
ADD	SUBTRACT	
FOR MOONSET		

II - TABLE OF CORRECTIONS FOR LATITUDES

FOR MOONRISE			
NORTH SUBTRACT		ADD	MINUTES TO ADD
SOUTH ADD		SUBTRACT	OR SUBTRACT
	ARIES	LIBRA	NONE
	TAURUS	SCORPIO	15
	GEMINI	SAGITTARIUS	25
	CANCER	CAPRICORN	35
	LEO	AQUARIUS	25
	VIRGO	PISCES	15
NORTH	ADD	SUBTRACT	
SOUTH	SUBTRACT	ADD	
FOR MOONSET			

Table 5   Correction Tables for Moonrise and Moonset

104

moon sign. Again, the correction depends on whether you are to the north or south of the middle of the country.

Although these corrections for latitude depend on the moon sign, they do not include the corrections that you would make for the moon sign seasons. Those must be considered separately.

Before making any corrections for the moon sign season or for the latitude, you must be sure that your moon phase age is accurate. One day of moon age error can cause a 50-minute difference in the time of moonrise or moonset (as well as moon noon!).

Where Is the Moon's Node This Year?

You saw earlier how the moon's influences depend on how far the tilt of the moon's orbit takes the moon from the earth's equator. The further from the equator, the greater the variability of the moon's influences during the days and over the weeks. You also saw that the tilt of the moon's orbit changes slowly over an 18.6-year cycle. The question is, how can you find out if you are being influenced by such a long-term moon cycle?

I have prepared Table 6 to help you find out. It is called the Moon Node Table. Before I describe it, let me refresh your memory about the moon's nodes and what they can tell you.

The Ascending Node is the point where the moon's orbit passes upward through the ecliptic plane. The moon and sun pull more strongly when they are lined up in the ecliptic plane at the nodes. Once you know the position of the Ascending Node you know a great deal about the moon's orbit. You know that the Descending Node, where the moon's orbit passes downward through the ecliptic plane, is on the opposite side of the zodiac from the Ascending Node. And you know that the moon's orbit is furthest below the ecliptic plane halfway between the Descending Node and the Ascending Node. You may recall from Chapter 2 that its position below the ecliptic plane determines how far the orbit will take the moon from the equator. And, as I just said, that determines the variability of the moon's influences.

105

Let me show you how the Moon Node Table can help you find the changing positions of the moon's nodes, and other important features of the moon's orbit.

Notice that the table consists of pairs of dates arranged in columns and rows, covering the period from March 1893 to December 2001. Each column covers an 18-year period, shown by the dates across the tops of the columns. Each row contains pairs of dates, each of which covers an 18-month interval of time. The rows are identified by signs of the zodiac in a column on the left side of the table. These signs are the Ascending and Descending Nodes of the moon's orbit during the 18-month intervals covered by the dates in each row. The Ascending Node is shown in large type, while the Descending Node is shown in smaller type.

If you look at the Moon Node Table, you can see, in the first row, that the moon's Ascending Node was in Aries from March 1893 to October 1894. The Descending Node was in Libra. The moon's nodes were in the same signs of the zodiac during all the other periods of time show by the dates along that first row.

To be sure that you know how to find the moon's nodes, try to find the Descending Node for the period from August 1978 to February 1980. It is in Pisces. You will find that pair of dates in the eighth row down. Remember, the Descending Node is the one that is in the smaller type in the left-hand column of nodes. (We will see how to use these moon node positions in the next chapter.)

There is more information in this Moon Node Table. The signs of the zodiac at the right-hand side of the table tell you where the moon's orbit is when it is furthest above or below the ecliptic plane. You recall from Chapter 2 that the moon's orbit makes its maximum tilt from the equator when it is furthest below the ecliptic in Capricorn. And it makes its minimum tilt from the equator when it is below the ecliptic in Cancer. These then are the severest and mildest moon seasons, respectively.

The column at the extreme right of the table describes the tilt of the moon's orbit from the equator in a numerical scale from 1 to 5, between its minimum and maximum tilt. The (+) or (−) sign following the nu-

106

MOON NODE TABLE

ASCENDING NODE / DESCENDING NODE	1893-1911	1911-1930	1930-1949	1949-1967	1967-1986	1986-2001	ABOVE ECLIPTIC / BELOW ECLIPTIC	TILT
♈ ARIES ♎ LIBRA	MAR 1893 / OCT 1894	DEC 1911 / JUN 1913	JUL 1930 / JAN 1932	MAR 1949 / AUG 1950	OCT 1967 / APR 1969	MAY 1986 / NOV 1987	CANCER ♋ / ♑ CAPRICORN	MAX.
♓ PISCES ♍ VIRGO	NOV 1894 / MAY 1896	JUL 1913 / DEC 1914	FEB 1932 / AUG 1933	SEP 1950 / MAR 1952	MAY 1969 / OCT 1970	DEC 1987 / JUN 1989	GEMINI ♊ / ♐ SAGITTARIUS	5(-)
♒ AQUARIUS ♌ LEO	JUN 1896 / NOV 1897	JAN 1915 / JUL 1916	SEP 1933 / FEB 1935	APR 1 52 / OCT 1953	NOV 1970 / MAY 1972	JUL 1989 / DEC 1990	TAURUS ♉ / ♏ SCORPIO	4(-)
♑ CAPRICORN ♋ CANCER	DEC 1897 / JUN 1899	AUG 1916 / JAN 1918	MAR 1935 / SEP 1936	NOV 1953 / APR 1955	JUN 1972 / DEC 1973	JAN 1991 / JUL 1992	ARIES ♈ / ♎ LIBRA	3(-)
♐ SAGITTARIUS ♊ GEMINI	JUL 1899 / JAN 1901	FEB 1918 / AUG 1919	OCT 1936 / MAR 1938	MAY 1955 / NOV 1956	JAN 1974 / JUN 1975	AUG 1992 / FEB 1994	PISCES ♓ / ♍ VIRGO	2(-)
♏ SCORPIO ♉ TAURUS	FEB 1901 / JUL 1902	SEP 1919 / MAR 1921	APR 1938 / OCT 1939	DEC 1956 / MAY 1958	JUL 1975 / JAN 1977	MAR 1994 / AUG 1995	AQUARIUS ♒ / ♌ LEO	1(-)
♎ LIBRA ♈ ARIES	AUG 1902 / FEB 1904	APR 1921 / SEP 1922	NOV 1939 / MAY 1941	JUN 1958 / DEC 1959	FEB 1977 / JUL 1978	SEP 1995 / MAR 1997	CAPRICORN ♑ / ♋ CANCER	MIN.
♍ VIRGO ♓ PISCES	MAR 1904 / SEP 1905	OCT 1922 / APR 1924	JUN 1941 / NOV 1942	JAN 1960 / JUL 1961	AUG 1978 / FEB 1980	APR 1997 / SEP 1998	SAGITTARIUS ♐ / ♊ GEMINI	1(+)
♌ LEO ♒ AQUARIUS	OCT 1905 / MAR 1907	MAY 1924 / NOV 1925	DEC 1942 / JUN 1944	AUG 1961 / JAN 1963	MAR 1980 / SEP 1981	OCT 1998 / APR 2000	SCORPIO ♏ / ♉ TAURUS	2(+)
♋ CANCER ♑ CAPRICORN	APR 1907 / OCT 1908	DEC 1925 / MAY 1927	JUL 1944 / DEC 1945	FEB 1963 / AUG 1964	OCT 1981 / MAR 1983	MAY 2000 / DEC 2001	LIBRA ♎ / ♈ ARIES	3(+)
♊ GEMINI ♐ SAGITTARIUS	NOV. 1908 / APR 1910	JUN 1927 / DEC 1928	JAN 1946 / JUL 1947	SEP 1964 / MAR 1966	APR 1983 / OCT 1984	- / -	VIRGO ♍ / ♓ PISCES	4(+)
♉ TAURUS ♏ SCORPIO	MAY 1910 / NOV 1911	JAN 1929 / JUN 1930	AUG 1947 / FEB 1949	APR 1966 / SEP 1967	NOV 1984 / APR 1986	- / -	LEO ♌ / ♒ AQUARIUS	5(+)

Table 6   Moon Node Table

107

merical tilt values tells you if the tilt is increasing (+) or decreasing (−) during the period of time covered by the dates on that row.

Again, we will see how to use this long-term feature of the moon's orbit when we get to Chapter 5.

How to Plot Moon Phases and Signs

You just saw how easy it is to find the moon's phases and signs for any date. The question is, what do you do with them after you find them? You know that you want to compare the moon position at your birthdate with its position at other special occasions. But how?

I am now going to show you how to plot moon phases and signs so that you can see, at a glance, if there are any meaningful patterns between them. You won't need special forms. Any pad of paper will do. However, if you have quarter-inch square-ruled paper, your plots will be easier to make and they will look neater.

Figure 4–3, the Moon Phase Plot, is used for comparing the phases of the moon on different dates.

If you look at the plot you will see that it consists of a listing of the moon's age, in days, counterclockwise around the sides of a square. Each side of the square represents a quadrant of the moon's orbit, as described in Chapter 3. These are the quadrants of waxing and waning light, and increasing or decreasing gravitational forces. The corners of the square represent the four major phases of the moon.

The annotated plot shown in the upper portion of the figure is not intended to be the one you work with. It is there to help you understand what the plot represents and to serve as a model if you want to use it to make up your own supply of blank forms of the Moon Phase Plot. In your own work you may prefer to prepare the simpler plot shown in the lower portion of the figure. In that case, you would write your numbers in a square as shown, without margins or notations.

Regardless of how fancy or how simple your Moon Phase Plot format is, you can use it to compare the moon's phase on one date with its phase on another date.

108

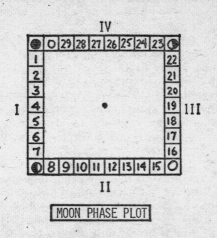

MOON PHASE PLOT

WORKING PLOT FOR FREDDIE PRINZE'S SUICIDE

Fig. 4-3   Moon Phase Plot

Let me show you how to do that by comparing the moon's phase on the day that Freddie Prinze shot himself with the moon phase on the day he was born. Here, we are comparing an event moon with a natal moon. You may recall that you found his natal moon phase had a moon age of 21 days. Notice that I have placed a dark crescent at the 21 on the Moon Phase Plot to show that it is a natal moon phase. The crescent represents the moon, not its phase. The darkened area signifies it as a natal moon.

Freddie Prinze shot himself on January 28, 1977. The moon's phase had a moon age of 8 days. I placed an open crescent near the number 8 on the Moon Phase Plot to show that as the event moon for that day.

It is often easier to see the relationship between moon phases when a line is drawn from the moon's positions to the center of the Moon Phase Plot. Notice that when I did that for the two moon positions on Freddie Prinze's chart, it shows that the event moon is at the opposite phase from his natal moon phase. You often see that pattern with unfortunate or unpleasant events.

I am not going to discuss the analysis of moon phase relationships here. I just wanted to show you how to make up a Moon Phase Plot and how to use it to see the relationships between moon phases on different dates. Later we will look into the ways to use the quadrant information.

Plotting Moon Signs

The Moon Sign Plot (Fig 4–4) is made up the same way that you make up the Moon Phase Plot. That is, by listing numbers around the sides of a square. However, in this case there are thirty-six numbers representing the decans that you find from the Decan Moon Sign Table (Table 4). Since that table gives you the sun signs as well as the moon signs, the Moon Sign Plot can be used to plot the relationships between sun signs along with the relationships between moon signs.

Notice that the decan numbers are arranged counterclockwise around the sides of the square so that there are three signs of the zodiac on each side. The upper portion of the figure shows how each side corresponds with

110

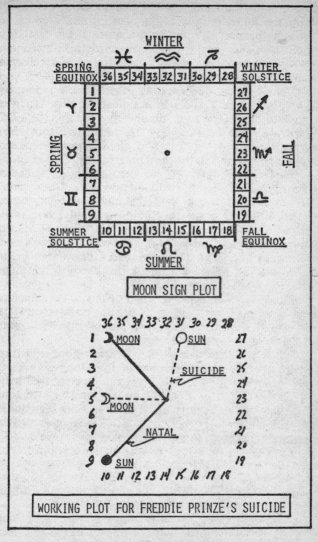

MOON SIGN PLOT

WORKING PLOT FOR FREDDIE PRINZE'S SUICIDE

Fig. 4–4 Moon Sign Plot

111

each of the four seasons. The corners of the square correspond with the equinoxes and the solstices, as shown. Again, the upper portion of the figure is not intended as a working plot unless you can reproduce it for your own supply of blank forms. The lower portion of the figure shows you how to prepare a working plot by numbering around the square in increments of nine steps each.

Let me show you how to use the Moon Sign Plot by showing you how Freddie Prinze's natal moon sign was related to the moon sign on the day he shot himself. Prinze was born on February 22, 1954, and shot himself on January 28, 1977. You already found that his natal moon sign was in the third decan of Pisces, decan 36.

I placed a darkened crescent moon near decan 36 on the Moon Sign Plot, in the lower part of the figure. The crescent is to represent the moon, not its phase. It is darkened to show that it is the natal moon. The event moon signs are represented by open crescents, as shown at decan 5 on the plot. That was the moon's sign for January 28, 1977. (You can check that decan number for yourself by using Table 4, the Decan Moon Sign Table, for January 28, 1977.)

I have also shown Freddie Prinze's natal sun sign along with the event sun sign, on this same plot. The natal sun is shown by a darkened full circle. The event sun sign is represented by an open circle.

When the natal sun sign and natal moon sign are connected by lines to the center of the Moon Sign Plot, a relationship is often revealed that can be compared with a similar set of lines drawn between the sun sign and moon sign of the event date. The angles between these lines fall into regular patterns which reveal unfavorable alignments that seem to accompany unpleasant events.

Let's take a look at how those alignments can tell us when the moon will bring bad days.

112

5
The Moon and Bad Times

Introduction

Here's where we begin using everything that we have learned up to now. You know that the moon's changing phases and signs bring about changes in your environment. Some of those changes affect you by the actions of fields and forces on your physical and psychological responses. Furthermore, those responses depend on how the sun and moon seasons compare with the seasons that were imprinted on you at the time of your birth.

In this chapter we will look at how natal conditions compare with the conditions during depressed moods, accidents, suicides, sickness and death, and other periods of difficulty. We will use the tables, charts and plotting methods that you learned about in Chapter 4. The question is, are there any general patterns that show up in the moon's positions whenever you are having one of those bad days? Let's see.

There are many reasons for people to get into the "dumps." The position of the moon may be one of them. Certain phases of the moon are related to increased ionization levels. The Full Moon produces an increase in positive ionization which in turn has been traced to increases in the production of serotonin, a mood-modifying body chemical. This neurohormone, which is produced in response to stress, is a "downer," while the adrenaline-like stress hormone norepinephrine, is an "upper." Perhaps, eons ago, the environment that stimulates the production of serotonin was an environment from which we were best advised to withdraw. And the depressed state it produced lead us into that appropriate withdrawal behavior.

The amount of serotonin that we produce in response to our environment differs from one person to the next. That may depend on your natal moon phase. It has been found that about one-quarter of the population is "weather sensitive" to these changes in ionization. This suggests that people who are born in one quadrant of the moon phase cycle are more prone to this sensitivity than those born under other natal phases. Only an extensive statistical study can tell.

Which moon phase bothers you the most? Few people ever notice the moon's phase, so they would hardly know which ones are more troublesome. However, if you have kept a diary, or can remember some particularly bad days, you can check them now. Let me show you the kinds of things to look for.

The first thing that you should look for is the phase of the moon. The chances are that when you are having a hard time, the moon is at a "hard" angle with respect to the position of your natal moon phase. There are four hard angles. These are "conjunctions" at 0 degrees, "oppositions" at 180 degrees, and two "squares," one at 90 degrees and the other at 270 degrees.

You can visualize these hard angles if you imagine that your natal moon was a New Moon. If the moon phase during some event, which we will call the event moon, was a New Moon, then it would be in conjunction with your natal moon. The angle between your natal moon and that event moon would be 0 degrees. If the moon was at its First Quarter, it would be square to your natal moon. The First Quarter Moon is 90 degrees from the New Moon. If the event moon was a Full Moon, it would be in opposition to your natal moon, since it would be 180 degrees away. The Last Quarter Moon, 270 degrees ahead of the New Moon is also 90 degrees behind it. That 90 degrees makes it square to your natal moon.

Bad times seem to come up whenever the event moon is at these hard angles to the natal moon. Not just the angles between the moon phases, but also the angles between the natal moon sign and the event moon sign. And beyond that, between the moon signs and the sun signs. It's as though your imprinting assumes that the natal moon is at one of the corners of the four moon phase quadrants, or the four moon seasons, and expects energy changes to occur at the other corners with respect to that natal corner. Since the event moon at those corners is not at a true energy change corner, something inside you is violated. Stresses then appear in their many discomforting ways.

Let's look at how some of these stresses show up on the Moon Sign and Moon Phase plots. We will look at the bad days in the lives of two women.

The first, Mildred, is an easy-going homemaker who is known to all her friends for her positive outlook and cheerful manner. But on October 14, 1978, she fell into a deep depression. She was especially concerned because she couldn't find any reason for it. She just felt depressed and wanted to be left alone.

The other woman, a young lady whom we will call Sophie, was having a hard time making her marriage work. She had four years of seemingly endless quarrels. On April 24, 1977, she gave her husband his final message. Shape up or ship out!

Let's plot the moon's positions for those dates and compare them with the natal positions of each one. The first step is to find the moon's phase for the event dates and for the birthdates of the two women, using Table 3, the Moon Phase Table, in Chapter 4.

Then, using the Decan Moon Sign Table (Table 4)

115

in Chapter 4, the next step is to find the moon signs on those same dates of interest: the event dates and the birthdates.* We will need the moon signs in terms of decan numbers so that we can plot them on the Moon Sign Plots (Fig 4–4), as shown in Chapter 4. While you are looking up the moon signs, you should also look up the sun signs for those same dates of interest. You'll see why in a minute.

Mildred's Moon Sign Plot and Moon Phase Plot are shown in Figure 5-1. Notice that this is a working plot, without the quadrant notations or season and sign notations that you saw in Chapter 4. This working plot shows you how you can use a typewriter to make up your blank forms for plotting. The only purpose of this plot is to reveal whether there are hard angles between event conditions and natal conditions.

Notice the darkened crescent and darkened full circle in the upper part of the figure. They represent Mildred's natal moon sign and sun sign, respectively. The solid lines drawn from those symbols to the center of the plot help you keep your eye on the relation between those natal conditions. The dotted line drawn from the open symbols to the center of the plot help you keep your eye on the sun and moon signs associated with the event dates represented by those symbols. In this case, those open symbols represent the sun and moon signs of October 14, 1978.

The darkened crescent in the lower part of the figure represents Mildred's natal moon phase. The open crescent is the moon's phase on October 14, 1978. It is at moon age 13 days, two days before a Full Moon.

Let's look at these plots to see what they can tell us.

Notice from the Moon Sign Plot, that on October 14 the moon was near Mildred's natal moon sign, while the sun was near the opposite sign. Two hard angles. The moon was in conjunction with her natal moon, and the sun was in opposition to her natal moon. The sun was in a position on October 14, 1978, that it would have been in during a Full Moon in the month of her birth. The natal

*You can practice on the event dates here, but I'll have to do the birthdates myself. If I told you when Mildred and Sophie were born they'd kill me.

116

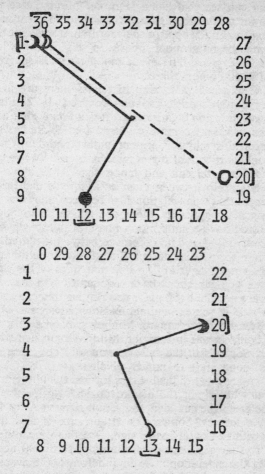

Fig. 5-1 Mildred's Bad Day

117

moon imprinting would have "remembered" the October 14 sun position as the Full Moon position nearest her birthdate.

You can see that again from the Moon Phase Plot in the lower part of the figure. Notice that the event moon is nearing the Full Moon. In that position, it makes a hard angle with the natal moon phase. In this case, the hard angle is 90 degrees. The event moon phase is square to Mildred's natal moon phase.

Now let's see what kind of angles there are in the plots for Sophie's crisis day on April 24, 1977. Figure 5-2 shows her Moon Sign Plot and Moon Phase Plot, using the same working formats we used for Mildred. Again the darkened symbols represent natal conditions, while open symbols represent the event conditions. You can see that Sophie's natal sun and moon signs have about the same relationship between them as Mildred's natal signs. You recall that the relationship between the sun and moon signs is shown by the moon phase. Both Sophie and Mildred have a natal moon phase of twenty days (in terms of moon age). The difference between Mildred and Sophie is in the seasons of their birth. You can tell that because their natal signs are on different sides of the Moon Sign Plot. You can check back to Chapter 4 to see which seasons are on which sides. Or you can just remember that the top side is winter, and the seasons advance counterclockwise around the square. Mildred's moon sign was in spring, Sophie's was in summer. Mildred's sun sign was in summer, Sophie's in the fall. As you plot your bad days you will soon start to notice which seasons of the sun and moon are more difficult times for you than others.

But what about those hard angles? Notice that the angle between the sun sign and moon sign on April 24 is about 90 degrees. Sophie's natal sun sign is also about square with her natal moon sign. But these are different kinds of squares. In one case, the natal sun is 90 degrees ahead of the natal moon. In the other case, the event sun is 270 degrees ahead of the event moon (or 90 degrees behind it).

These opposite-type squares in the sun and moon signs cause the event moon phase to be at a hard angle, in opposition, to the natal moon phase.

118

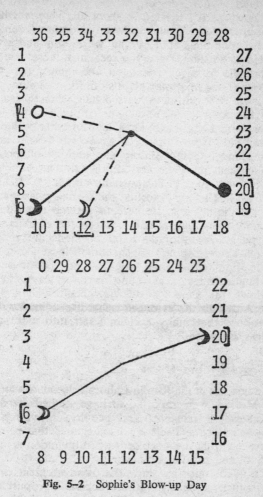

Fig. 5-2 Sophie's Blow-up Day

119

There are too many combinations of natal conditions and event conditions for me to describe which combinations lead to hard angles, or the kinds of hard angles they lead to. All I wanted to show you here was how to begin noticing the angles between your natal conditions and the conditions that prevail when you find yourself in a depressed state. Once you recognize those angles you will be able to check ahead on upcoming moon phases and signs to see what may be in store for you. Somehow, it is easier to cope with a depressed state when you can find some reason for it.

Now that you have some idea of what to look for, try two plots for yourself. I have two more dates for Mildred and Sophie. Mildred had another of those bad spells earlier, on February 22, 1977. And Sophie had a major blow-up with her husband on May 6, 1977. Use the tables in Chapter 4 to find the moon's phases and the signs for those dates. Be sure to get the sun signs too. Then plot those phases and signs on the charts with the natal positions. Mildred's natal positions are shown in Figure 5-1, and Sophie's are shown in Figure 5-2.

It shouldn't surprise you to find that these same hard angles can also be found on those days when you fall down the steps or cut your hand with a kitchen knife. Although the evidence is hard to come by, there's little doubt that many accidents fall into moon-related patterns. Let's see.

Accidents by the Moon

Scientists at the Sandia Laboratories in Albuquerque, New Mexico, were reported to have studied the correlations between accidents and geophysical variables for over twenty years. Their results suggested that people are more likely to have an accident when the moon is in opposition to their natal moon phase.

Russian statistics show that road accidents increase by as much as four times the normal rate, just after a major solar flare eruption. The flares put forth intense ultraviolet radiation which in turn increases the ionization levels in our atmosphere. Those higher levels have been found to slow down human reaction times. Slower reaction times of course mean more accidents. You hit the brakes too late.

But we don't have to wait for solar flares to experience changes in our ionization levels. The moon affects those ionization levels, less dramatically but more regularly, with the changing phases of the moon. If the Sandia study was correct, then it tells us that our responses to those different ionization levels may depend on our natal moon phase. Let's look at some accidents to see how the event moons relate to the natal moons of the accident victims.

Consider the late Bing Crosby. He fell from a stage during a performance on March 3, 1977. Bing Crosby was born on May 2, 1904. He died on October 14, 1977. When you look up the phases and signs for those dates and plot them on the Moon Sign and Moon Phase plots, you will find the patterns as shown in Figure 5-3. It shows the day he fell from the stage.

I used this example to show you that you can have a bad day without a hard angle on the Moon Phase Plot. In this case the moon's phase was one day before a Full Moon. Many accidents occur near a Full Moon, perhaps because the ionization levels are higher. But then too, it seems that those conditions will affect you differently, depending on whether there are hard angles between the zodiac positions of the sun and moon. Notice in the figure that the event sun sign and event moon sign are in opposition to each other. But that is just another way of saying that there is a Full Moon. However, both the event sun and event moon signs are at hard angles with respect to the natal moon. They are both square. It may be that these hard angles set up by the event signs set up your susceptibility to the influences of the Full Moon.

If you look up the event conditions for the day Crosby died you will see that the moon phase was in opposition to his natal moon phase. The event moon sign was in opposition to the natal sun sign, while his natal moon sign was in square to the event sun sign. Plot it and see. Death may be the final accident in life. We will look at the phases and signs that accompany illness and death, later in this chapter.

121

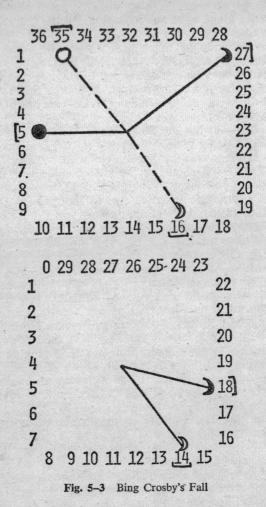

Fig. 5-3 Bing Crosby's Fall

122

Accidents which fall at the Full Moon generally are accompanied by these hard angles between the natal signs and the event signs. But sometimes other factors enter.

Consider the following accident that happened to someone close to me. She was born May 26, 1936 (not shy about her age). On February 13, 1976, she had a bad fall. If you plot those positions you will find the Full Moon, but no hard angle with the natal moon phase. However, the event sun is in opposition with her natal moon, and the event moon is square to her natal sun. Later, when I pointed that out to her, she smiled and said that I forgot the most important factor. "Mort," she smiled, "it was Friday the thirteenth!"

And indeed, if you expect an accident, you might invite one. Which brings up an important point. When you start finding the different patterns of phases and signs that seem to go with your bad days, you must use those findings wisely. Those patterns do not cause the bad times. They represent the conditions under which the unpleasant things are more likely to occur. Once you know that, you can compensate for them by, say, an increased alertness to offset a reduced reaction time. The patterns tell you when the conditions might make accidents more likely. But not inevitable! To be forewarned is to be forearmed.

Let me give you the dates of a few accidents so that you can get some practice in plotting them and in spotting the hard angles and the Full Moons. On July 17, 1977, one of my relatives tripped over a chair at a pool and badly wrenched her shoulder. It was at about 10:30 P.M., Daylight Saving Time. I tell you that so you can get some experience with the Daily Moon Chart (Fig. 4-2) to see where the moon was when she fell. You should find that the moon had just set. (Don't forget to add the 1½-hour correction for the moon sign when you use Table 5.) Then, about a week later, a jar broke and cut her on the wrist. That was on July 28, 1977. You will need her natal conditions, which you find from her birthday, January 3, 1930.

Another, more tragic, accident occurred on August 28, 1977. A relative drove her car into a tree and was killed. No one was with her, and no one was on the

123

road. She was born on February 7, 1926, one day before a Full Moon.

As you begin working with these patterns you will see some that seem to show up again and again on the bad days. You see them when you have bad moods, fights, accidents, and even in suicides. You may have noticed it when we plotted the event conditions for Freddie Prinze's suicide.

Suicide by the Moon

People who are especially prone to the forces which bring on depressions may be spending so much time in depressed states that they fall into suicidal despair. And then, when the moon brings in that "extra straw" of increased ionization, it may pull the trigger of that suicidal impulse.

That triggering effect of increased ionization can be seen more easily in the suicide rates which rise sharply when the Witches' Winds blow. These are the warm, dry winds which carry positive ions with them as they fall after crossing mountains. Switzerland has its Foehn; France, its Mistral; Italy, its Sirocco; Israel, its Sharav (or Hamsin); and we have the California Santa Ana, and the Northwest Chinook. Records clearly show that suicides, murders, and other acts of violence will rise as these winds rise.

Again, the moon brings these same effects as the winds, less dramatically but more regularly, as it causes periodic changes in the ionization levels of our atmosphere.

Let's look at a typical plot of a suicide. It is typical in the pattern between the signs and phases, but not typical in the event conditions. Most suicide attempts are made in February and March (Pisces and Aries), by people who are born in May (Taurus and Gemini). Figure 5-4 shows the plots for the day a 22-year-old girl committed suicide. Notice that although her natal sign was in Gemini, the event sun was in opposition to the signs of Pisces and Aries, the signs in which most suicides are attempted.

You can see in the figure that there were hard an-

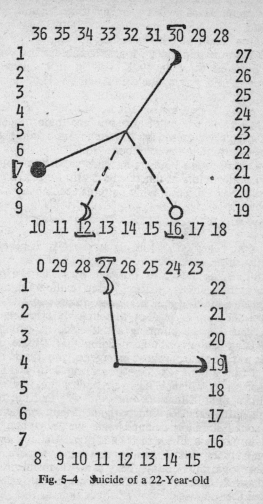

Fig. 5-4   Suicide of a 22-Year-Old

125

gles in the signs and the phases. The event moon was in opposition to her natal moon. The event sun was in square to her natal sun. The event phase was square to her natal moon phase. Hard angles and hard times seem to go hand in hand.

You might find it interesting to plot the conditions on the day that Marilyn Monroe committed suicide. She was born on June 1, 1926, still in that suicide-prone Taurus-Gemini group. She died August 5, 1962. The event moon phase was in opposition to her natal moon phase. You will also find a near square and near opposition in her Moon Sign Plot of the sun and moon signs. Her natal moon is opposed by the event sun, while her natal sun is square to the event moon.

Suicide is an illness that ends in death. Let's look now at other plots of illness and death. One of the major killers is heart disease. What patterns accompany it?

Heart Attacks and Death

Your heart is about as big as your fist. It beats about seventy times each minute. During that minute your entire blood supply passes through your heart. However, when a threatening situation arises, calling for a "flight or fight" response, your heart can pump about five times its normal output. It does that first by speeding up its beat, and then by pumping about twice its volume with each beat. But it can't keep doing that all the time. It needs to recover from those emergency situations.

Today's complex life-styles bring with them a pattern of stress which affects our bodies the way that the "flight or fight" situations once did. We find ourselves in hostile circumstances which signal "flight or fight," yet our social situation demands that we "stay and smile." And so our hearts beat faster and strain against unnatural circumstances. Little wonder that heart attacks are the number one killer today. They are responsible for more deaths than cancer, strokes, accidents, pneumonia or the other killer diseases.

And little wonder that heart attacks rise sharply when the Witches' Winds begin to blow. Those winds, with their positive ions, cause increased flows of the stress hormones. These then trigger our stress responses even though, in this case, the stresses are caused by invisible ions. Increased heart action is one such response to those stresses.

You recall that the moon phases produce regular patterns of change in our environment that stimulate the production of serotonin, the stress hormone. And so we can expect that heart attacks will follow the phases of the moon. And again, they do so, depending on the susceptibility of the person, as determined by his natal conditions. Let's look at some heart attacks and see how the natal conditions and event conditions are related.

Figure 5-5 shows the Moon Phase and Moon Sign plots for the day that a young man had his first heart attack. The date was May 31, 1969. Notice that there was a Full Moon that day. Full Moons and increased ionization levels go hand in hand. Notice also that the Full Moon was at a hard angle to his natal moon phase. It was square. In this case there were no hard angles in the Moon Sign Plot, other than a near conjunction between the natal moon sign and the event moon sign.

This man had another attack about seven years later, on September 21, 1976. That attack cost him his life. It struck him at his desk at work. He just keeled over. If you plot the conditions on that date you will find that the event sun and the event moon were near a conjunction. That would place the event moon near a New Moon, just opposite the moon phase at his first attack.

That pattern is almost identical with the pattern you will find if you plot the first heart attack of Clark Gable and compare it with the conditions on the day he died of a second heart attack. Clark Gable was born on February 1, 1901. He had a major heart attack on November 5, 1960. The moon was just past the Full Moon. It was in conjunction with his natal moon. The event sun was square to his natal sun, and almost square with his natal moon.

Eleven days later, on November 16, 1960, he had another attack and died. The event sun and event moon signs were almost in conjunction. It was almost a New Moon on the day he died.

Unfortunately, there is a good chance that you know of someone who has had a heart attack, or succumbed to

127

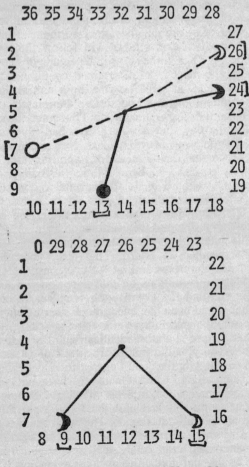

Fig. 5-5 Heart Attack of Young Man

one. If you know their birthdates and the dates of their attacks, you can plot the natal and event conditions to see the patterns that accompany these unfortunate circumstances. You will soon see these patterns of hard angles and event moons in opposition on the dates of attacks and deaths. In many of these cases there seems to be a fatal moon as well as a natal moon.

Following the Longer Tides

Up to now we have been looking at bad times in terms of the hard angles between the moon phases and the signs of event dates as compared with the natal conditions. But there are longer cycles of lunar effects which produce good periods or more difficult periods throughout our lives. These periods are related to the longer-term cycles in the tilt of the moon's orbit. As the tilt changes from its position at the time of our birth, it brings with it changes in the severity of the moon seasons. Throughout life we find ourselves in periods of decreasing or increasing seasonal severity, depending on the season of our birth. And that affects how we respond to our life situations.

It is difficult to remember the status of our lives from one period in this 18.6-year cycle to another. Our memories do not serve us well over such long periods. However, if you can look back over your life and identify the "up" times and the "down" times, you may find interesting correlations between those times and the changing tilt of the moon's orbit. Let's look at one case to show you how you can explore the moon's role in your own past, and possible future.

A middle-aged executive, born in November 1924, reviewed his career in search of possible patterns that might reveal a trend in upcoming activities. He recalled that his years of study, in the late 1940s, were marked by vigor and vitality. Not surprising. The 1950s were the career development years, marked by unrest and frequent changes. Again, not too unusual. Then a major growth period began in the early 1960s which lasted until the early 1970s. Then things began to slow down until about 1977, after which there seemed to be a renewed enthusiasm for expansive growth.

129

The question arises, is there anything in the long-term moon-cycle pattern that might be related to this long-term career trend? Let's see.

Look at the Moon Node Table (Table 6) in Chapter 4. It tells us the moon's orbital tilt over the years. Notice that the tilt was $2(+)$ in November 1924, the year of his birth. That would represent the severity of the moon season at the time of his natal imprinting. During his years of study in the 1940s, the orbit's tilt was growing from $2(+)$ to $5(+)$. The moon seasons were getting more severe and variable and reached maximum severity in the early 1950s.

The disturbances accompanying his career development years occurred during the time that the moon's orbit was moving from its maximum value toward its minimum value in 1959. In 1959 his dissatisfaction was so great that he moved his family to another area to change his job conditions. Things picked up, and in 1963, when the moon's orbit moved into a $2(+)$ tilt, his natal condition, he launched out into his own business, which grew and prospered until 1970. At that time the moon's orbit had just passed its maximum tilt again and was now at $5(-)$. From then on, things slid down slowly until late 1977. And then new ventures were sought out and pursued with enthusiasm, starting in mid-1978.

If the long-term pattern repeats itself, this person can expect that the next decade will provide the forces and energies of the moon seasons that were so favorable for him during the late 1940s and again in the late 1960s. Things are looking up for him.

That is not to say that everyone responds to those tilts and their seasons in the same way. Had he been born in a $3(-)$ year, the *changes* from those natal conditions would probably have more influence than the actual values of the orbital tilts. In other words, it may not be the value of the tilt as much as it is the way the tilt changes from the time you were imprinted by the season of your birth.

It did occur to me, however, that if the absolute value of the orbital tilt makes a difference in a person's approach to life, then it may help to explain the eternal

130

generation gap. People born 25 years apart must enter the moon's tilt cycle at different points which then influence them to become different from their parents. They are more likely to be the same as a 37-year-old person, or a 56-year-old person (multiples of 18.6).

This example is intended to show how you might explore the longer-range patterns in your life. Major changes may be linked to the changing tilt of the moon's orbit with respect to your natal tilt. Remember, I am offering these as speculations rather than dogmatic beliefs in how the moon can be influencing your life. You just have to try it for yourself to see if it works for you.

Let's turn now to see how the natal conditions of two people can be examined to tell us something about whether they will have problems in getting along with each other.

6
The Moon and Compatibility

Introduction

You have just seen how the moon's positions can bring about stressful conditions that affect your emotional and physical responses. It all depends on where the moon is with respect to your natal moon position. These stresses arrive in a monthly pattern as the moon moves through its conjunctions, squares and oppositions with respect to your natal moon. The way you respond to each of these hard angles depends on the season of your birth and how you learned to deal with the stresses brought by those hard angles. Some people become moody and outwardly irritable, while others withdraw into a silent indifference.

When two people spend a great deal of time together, they become part of each other's environment. The behavior of a woman, in response to her own stresses, becomes the environment of her partner. If that behavior is "up," then her partner experiences a favorable environment. However, if her behavior is "down," and difficult, then her partner will experience an uptight environment during that period of time.

And of course it works both ways. The compatibility between two people depends on how their individual monthly cycles overlap. And how they respond to their cycles. That will depend on their natal seasons of birth. Let's see how.

The Hard Natal Angles

When the moon is at a hard angle to your natal moon it means that it is at 0 degrees, 90 degrees or 180 degrees from your natal moon phase or moon sign. Now suppose that your companion's natal moon is at a hard angle to your natal moon. That means that when the event moon is at a hard angle to your natal moon, it is also at a hard angle to your companion's natal moon. You would both experience a stressed condition at the same time. A good example of that problem can be seen in the Moon Phase and Moon Sign plots of Farrah Fawcett-Majors and Lee Majors. Figure 6-1 shows these plots for their natal conditions.

On these plots the symbols show only the natal conditions. We are interested in the patterns between them rather than with the patterns with respect to an event day. The darkened symbols represent Farrah's natal conditions, while the open symbols represent Lee Majors' natal conditions. Farrah Leni Fawcett-Majors was born on February 2, 1947. Lee Majors was born on April 23, 1941. I have added a (+) to Farrah's symbols, and an arrow to Lee's symbols, to designate female and male, respectively. The crescent still represents the moon, and the circle represents the sun.

Notice first on the Moon Phase Plot that their natal moon phases are at a hard angle. They are 180 degrees apart, or, in opposition. Let's see what that combination of natal phases means. Let's say that on a particular day the event moon is in opposition to Farrah's natal moon. You can see that it will then be in conjunction with Lee's natal moon phase at the same time. Similarly, when a moon phase is in opposition to Lee's natal phase, it will be in conjunction with Farrah's natal phase.

The same problem comes up when an event moon is square to either natal moon phase. When an event moon

133

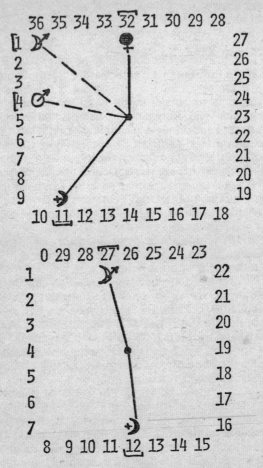

Fig. 6–1 Natal Chart of Lee Majors and Farrah Fawcett-Majors

134

is square to Lee's natal phase, say at a moon age of 4 days, it will also be square to Farrah's natal phase. That would happen again when the moon's age is 19 days. Check Figure 6-1 to see how that works out. When an event moon is in either of those positions it will stress both of them at the same time. Such an overlap of lunar stresses, which can be seen from a plot of their natal conditions, makes it difficult to maintain a harmonious relationship, since both people are "down" at the same time.

Nor do things get better for Farrah and Lee on the Moon Sign Plot. Notice that Farrah's natal moon sign is square to Lee's moon sign, and that their sun signs are also square to each other. When an event moon sign is in opposition to or conjunction with Lee's natal moon sign, it will then be square to Farrah's natal moon sign. And vice versa.

You can see another example of hard angles between the natal signs of Elizabeth Taylor and Richard Burton. Elizabeth Taylor was born on February 27, 1932. Richard Burton was born on November 11, 1925. If you plot their charts you will find that the Moon Phase Plot seems fine. However, the Moon Sign Plot shows a near conjunction and a near opposition between their natal suns and moons. If, for example, an event moon is at the Taurus-Gemini cusp, it would be square to Elizabeth's sun sign and to Burton's moon sign. It would, at the same time, be in conjunction with her moon sign and in opposition to his sun sign. Again, the overlapping of all the hard angles at the same time brings with it overlapping stresses for both people at the same time.

You may want to try another example for yourself. The plots of Sonny and Cher show a near opposition on the Moon Phase Plot. There is also a near conjunction between their sun and moon signs, which are approximately square to each other. You can plot their natal conditions to see how those near hard angles look. Sonny was born on February 16, 1940. Cher was born on May 20, 1946.

There are too many combinations of natal conditions between two people for me to describe them all. Or to

135

show you how each combination brings about mutual stress conditions when the moon moves through the various hard angles with respect to these natal conditions. However, as you begin to plot these natal conditions for your companions, you will see certain patterns between you and your compatible friends, and different patterns between you and those you try to avoid. And, with some practice, you will be able to spot potentially difficult periods when stresses can arise between you and your companions. Let me show you how to do that.

Spotting Upcoming Problem Days Between Partners

The problem days with partners occur when the moon is at a hard angle with respect to each of their natal moons. Let's use the plots for Farrah Fawcett-Majors and Lee Majors to see how to predict when such doubly difficult days would come up. First, we will find the dates when the moon phase will be at hard angles with their natal moon phases.

Farrah's natal moon phase has a moon age of 12 days, which is in opposition to Lee's natal moon phase of 27 days. Whenever the moon is at either of those ages it introduces a potential problem day for them. Also, moon ages of 4 days and 19 days would pose problems, since the moon would then be square to each of their natal moons at the same time. You can see that from the plot, or you can add or subtract 7 and 15 days to their natal moon phases. That would place the moon about one-quarter or one-half of the cycle from their natal phases.

When will the moon be at these hard angles of 4, 12, 19 and 27 days? You can use the Moon Phase Table (Table 3) in Chapter 4 to find out. First you must select a year and month for which you want to make your prediction. Let's say that Farrah wants to know when to be especially cautious during the month of September 1979.

The Moon Phase Table, Part I, tells her that September 1979 is shown in row E in Part II of the table. In row E she can then find the days in September corre-

136

sponding with the moon's ages listed across the top of the table. For example, in row E she would find that the date corresponding with a moon age of 4 days is the twenty-fourth of September. In that same row she would find that the date for a moon age of 12 days is September 2. In the same way, she would find the other dates in September 1979 at which the moon's phases would be at a hard angle with her natal phases and Lee's natal phases. Those dates turn out to be September 2 (moon age 12 days), September 9 (moon age 19 days), September 17 (moon age 27 days) and September 24 (moon age 4 days).

As a matter of procedure, you should first list the moon ages of interest, and then hold a straightedge across the row representing your month of interest. Then look across the top row of moon ages for the ages you want. When you find one, look down that column until you get to the straightedge, and then read the date of the month you find on that line.

As an alternative procedure, you can look up the dates of the major moon phases for the month of interest. Then you can write those dates at the corners of the Moon Phase Plot. You may then use those corner dates as reference points to find the dates of any moon phases that fall between those corner points.

Once you have found the dates of the phases that make hard angles with the natal phases, you can be more alert on those dates to avoid overreactions to the circumstances that may arise. Again, forewarned is forearmed.

You may also want to predict when the hard angles will come up with respect to the moon signs. Look again at Figure 6-1 to see how an event moon in decans 1 and 11 can cause problem days. The other signs that make hard angles with decans 1 and 11 are decans 19 and 29. You can spot those decans from the plot, or just add 9 and 18 to the natal signs. These would be the number of decans that will take you to one-quarter, and one-half, of the zodiac from the natal signs. That would place you at the hard angles of 90 degrees and 180 degrees from the natal signs, respectively.

Once you know which decans make the hard angles

with respect to your natal signs, you can find the dates that the moon will enter those decans. You will have to use the Decan Moon Sign Table (Table 4) along with the Moon Phase Table.

The easiest way to find the dates for the moon signs in any month is to find the date of the New Moon for that month. In Farrah Fawcett-Majors' case, she would be interested in the dates of the moon signs in September 1979. You recall that you would use row E of the Moon Phase Table to find the dates of the moon ages for September 1979. If you look at the table you will see that the New Moon occurs on September 20. Then, using the Decan Moon Sign Table, you can see that the New Moon on September 20 is in decan 18. Therefore, on the Moon Sign Plot, you can write September 20 next to decan 18. That establishes one date for a moon sign during that month.

You remember that the moon takes about 2½ days to move through each sign of the zodiac. That means that it moves through three decans in 2½ days, since there are three decans for each sign of the zodiac. Six decans would therefore represent 5 days. That means that you can count off six decans from your first decan, in this case decan 18, and identify it as September 25. That would show that the moon would enter decan 24 5 days after it entered decan 18. Continue identifying every sixth decan with a date that is 5 days beyond the previous date, until you have gone around the four sides of the Moon Sign Plot. Since you will have counted off only 30 days in this manner, you will be a day off in those months having 31 days. But that is close enough for the purposes of this kind of prediction.

Once you have the sides of the Moon Sign Plot marked off with the dates of the month, you can find the decans that make the hard angles and check off their dates to see when the moon enters those signs. In Farrah's case, the moon will be at hard angles to the natal moon signs on September 2, 9, 17 and 24. The dates for the hard angles with the moon's phases were September 6, 14, 21, and 29. If it turned out that the dates of hard angles for the signs and phases coincided, it would indicate that those overlapping dates are especially likely to bring on a

138

stressful test of the compatibility between Farrah and Lee.

There is another way you can estimate your compatibility with someone else, without having to check on the hard angles between your natal signs and phases. It still makes a comparison of your natal conditions. However, in this case it is a comparison of the seasons of your birth and the major quadrants of your natal moon phases during that season. This is how it works.

The Seasons of Compatibility

A recent study conducted in the Netherlands examined the question of whether birthdates have an influence on the choice of partners in marriage. The birthdates of over three thousand married couples were analyzed. Comparisons were made between their birth months to see if any combinations showed up more than others. The assumption was that if they got married, they had an initial preference for one another. The results were interesting. If you translate the birth months into the signs of the corresponding sun seasons, here is what you would find.

Women prefer men who are born about one season ahead of their own season of birth. For example, women born in early fall and mid-fall (Libra and Scorpio) marry men born in early winter and mid-winter (Capricorn and Aquarius) more often than would be expected by chance. The exception to this finding is with women who are born in early and mid-summer (Cancer and Leo). They prefer men born just before them in late spring and early summer (Gemini and Cancer).

Women divorce men who are born about one season behind their own season of birth. For example, women born in late spring (Gemini) have more divorces when they are married to men born in late winter (Pisces).

Of course this is only one study among many that have sought to discover how the seasons of birth may influence your life. While they may differ in specific findings, these studies agree that your life bears the imprint of the season of your birth. The Netherlands study concluded, ". . . partner choice in marriage is affected by the month of birth or some factor that is correlated

139

with the month of birth, so that partner choice seems to be predictable to some degree, only on the basis of month of birth."

It shouldn't really surprise you that the season of your birth can affect the way you approach things in life. People born in different seasons develop different responses to the changing environments brought by the changing sun signs and moon signs. Those responses, depending as they do on your natal signs, become the basis of your personality and determine the style with which you meet life's problems. Of course, all that is strongly influenced by the kind of adult guidance that goes into your formative years.

Therefore, it shouldn't be surprising that personalities born of different sun and moon seasons would find themselves at different levels of compatibility with each other, depending on their respective seasons of birth. For example, you might prefer people whose natal signs are a season ahead of yours, while others whose signs are close to your own make you feel uneasy. You won't be able to find that out from a statistical study. You are not a statistic. The only way to find out is to check the natal signs of all the people you know and then compare those signs with your own. You will soon see which signs are compatible with your own, and which you should treat with care. Let me show you how to do that.

There are really two seasons of your birth. The first is the familiar sun season, as shown by your natal sun sign. The second is the less familiar moon season, as shown by your natal moon sign. If we consider your season of birth in terms of your natal sun sign and moon sign, we would have to consider 144 different combinations of those twelve sun signs and twelve moon signs. However, if we consider your season of birth in terms of the traditional four seasons, we only have to deal with 16 combinations; four sun seasons times four moon seasons.

There is an easy way to plot the natal seasons of two people so that you can see how the moon was affecting their environment at the times of their birth. All you have to do is plot the natal moon season against the natal moon phase as shown in the table below.

140

	Moon Signs and Moon Seasons			
Moon Phase	CAPRICORN AQUARIUS PISCES	ARIES TAURUS GEMINI	CANCER LEO VIRGO	LIBRA SCORPIO SAGITTARIUS
	Winter	Spring	Summer	Fall
Quadrant I				
Quadrant II				
Quadrant III				
Quadrant IV				

Table 7 Plotting Natal Seasons of Two People

The columns in the table represent the moon signs and their corresponding moon seasons. The rows represent the moon phase, in terms of the quadrants, as described in Chapter 3. You recall that those quadrants tell you how the gravitational forces and electromagnetic energies are waxing and waning when the moon is passing through those quadrants.

You use this table by placing a mark in the appropriate column and row representing your natal moon season and moon phase, respectively. Then, having identified your own position among those sixteen locations, you place your friends into the locations corresponding with their natal moon signs and moon phases. The Moon Phase Table and Moon Sign Table (Tables 3 and 4) in Chapter 4 are used to find those natal conditions from your friends' birthdates. You should plot one set of friends with whom you enjoy compatible relationships, on one such table, while plotting your less agreeable friends on another table. You should see a definite difference in the two tables!

You might be wondering how this table, using only the moon sign and moon phase, can reflect the sun's season in this plot of your season of birth. But remember, the moon's phase depends on the relationshp between the moon sign and the sun sign. If you know the moon sign and the moon phase, it tells you the sun's sign. You could have made up a table of sun signs against moon signs. But

141

then you wouldn't see how the moon's changing phases are affecting the environment.

A final word before moving on to how the moon especially influences women.

The comparison between your natal season of birth and the natal seasons of your partners did not account for a possible difference in the severity of those moon seasons. Two people can be born in the same moon season, but the difference in the severity of those seasons would depend on the year in the 18.6-year Metonic cycle. That severity can make an interesting difference in how you relate to someone else's natal conditions.

One way to check that out is to find the Ascending Node of the moon's orbit at the time of your birth. Use the Moon Node Table (Table 6) in Chapter 4. Then you should find the Ascending Nodes for the birthdates of your companions. Once you have them, plot them on a Moon Sign Plot just as though they were a moon sign or sun sign. You can then look for patterns in the angles between their Ascending Nodes and your own. Be especially alert for those hard angles!

Let's move on now to see how the moon can have special effects on women.

7
The Moon and Women

Introduction

When you think about it, it's only natural that sexual activity and fertility should be related to the seasons. During our evolution, those who were born into hostile seasons were less likely to survive that environment. Those who were conceived at a time when they would be delivered into a fruitful season were more likely to survive. And more likely to repeat that successful pattern of sexual behavior.

Humans have since become more adaptable creatures so that we are no longer at the mercy of the harsh elements of the weather. However, there is still evidence of seasonal patterns in human sexuality. And those include the monthly seasons as well as the annual seasons. Something in the environment still turns us on and off with the changing phases of the moon and with the changing moon signs and their seasons.

Let's take a look at some of these seasonal effects on sexual activities as they affect the reproduction of life.

On Becoming a Woman—Menstruation

The onset of menstruation marks the beginning of womanhood. The regulation of this function and its companion functions of ovulation, conception and delivery are dependent upon partially understood chemical and psychological mechanisms. Nor do we fully understand the emotional states and moods that are linked to those basic functions. However, there is little doubt that these mechanisms are synchronized by environmental factors such as light, odors, electric fields and other geophysical forces. It is no wonder then that there are seasonal patterns to be found in menstrual cycles.

Let's take a quick look at some of these patterns. Perhaps they can help you recognize that your own experiences are not as unusual as you might have thought.

Most girls have their first period at the age of 13, although the ages vary from 11 to 15, depending in part on where you live. City girls mature about a half year earlier than rural girls, while girls in the tropics mature later. The menarche, or first period, is more likely to occur around the winter solstice, from November through January. It is less likely to occur during the Spring Equinox, from February to April.

Menstrual periods can be regular or irregular, depending on many factors having to do with neurohormonal mechanisms and their responses to environmental disturbances. In general, about a third of women have a regularity to within two days of their average period interval. About one-half of the women are regular to within four days of their average cycles. The remaining one fourth of women are irregular to the extent of being more than four days from their expected dates for the onset of menstruation.

But what is the "normal" time between the onset of successive menstruations? Most people will tell you that it is 28 days, give or take a day or so, suggesting that it is related to the lunar month. In fact, it is related to the lunar month, but it is not 28 days. There are several ways to measure the lunar month. A sidereal month of 27.322 days measures the time it takes for the moon to go around the earth once, back to its starting position in the zodiac. A synodic month of 29.5 days measures the time it takes to go around the earth once from one New Moon to the next New Moon. You may recall from Chapter 2 that the moon has to catch up with the moving sun to reach its position for the next New Moon. That takes longer.

The idea of a 28-day lunar month comes from the attempt to average the sidereal and synodic months. There are other measures of lunar months as well: 27.55 days from perigee to perigee, 27.21 days from node crossing to next node crossing, etc. But it turns out that the synodic month is the one that figures in the cycles of female sexual functions. Please remember that the synodic month can vary from 27 to 30 days, depending on the time of year; 29.5 days is the average.

Let's see now how it relates to female functions.

The menstrual cycle is the basis for the female reproductive cycle. There are several rules of thumb for determining the duration of a pregnancy, based on the start of the last menstrual cycle before conception. Ovulation, and therefore conception, occurs about halfway through the menstrual cycle (for most women). The authorities agree that it takes 266 days from the time of conception to delivery. However, since few people would know the dates of conception, the rules are tied to the onset of the last menses.

One rule suggests that you add 1 year to the date of the start of your last period, subtract 3 months and add 7 days. That would come to about 281 days. Another rule, obviously allowing for errors in recalling the dates of the last period, suggests that delivery can be expected 280 days after the last period, plus or minus 14 days (half the menstrual cycle). How do these rules relate to the synodic month of 29.5 days?

Biblical tradition places the term of pregnancy at nine months. They would be lunar months. Nine lunar months of 29.5 days each would come to 265.5 days, or 266 days. It seems that Biblical rules were based on timing pregnancies from the moment of conception. Suppose, instead, that they had decided to time pregnancies from the time of the start of the last menstrual cycle. They would have added another half month to allow for the

145

fact that ovulation occurs about a half month after the start of the menstrual cycle. Counting off 9.5 months from the last period would be 280.25 days! Those would be synodic lunar months of 29.5 days each.

It seems that the menstrual cycle is tied to the moon, and in particular to the synodic month. Remember, the 29.5 days represent an annual average for the synodic month. It can vary from 27 to 30 days, introducing similar variability in the "regularity" of menstrual cycles. The linkage of the menstrual cycle to the phase of the moon in the synodic month can be detected by other interesting relationships between the moon's phase and menstrual cycles.

The light of the moon may have been the synchronizer of menstrual cycles—in particular, the light of the Full Moon. If evolution preferred births by the Full Moon, then ovulation and conception would have occurred nine synodic months earlier, under a Full Moon. Menstruation would then have begun under a New Moon. Recent evidence suggests that irregular menstrual cycles can be reset to a lunar cycle by imitating the light of the Full Moon. Indeed, the imitation of the moon by the completely irregular pattern of night lighting may be responsible for most irregularities in the first place.

Women who have had histories of irregular menstrual cycles have been able to normalize their cycles by placing a small light in their bedrooms at night. The light is turned on to imitate the Full Moon during certain days of the menstrual cycle. It works like this.

Imagine that the first day of your menstrual cycle occurs at a New Moon. Don't wait for a New Moon. Just assume that your first flow marks the New Moon. Then, each night for 14 days, sleep in the dark. Pitch dark. That would take you to the time of a Full Moon if your period really started at a New Moon. Then, sleep for the next 3 nights with the small light left on all night. After that, return to sleeping in the dark. Counting the day of the first flow as day 1, you sleep with the light on during day 14, day 15 and day 16. Your cycles should then return to a regular pattern, and be 29 days apart.

However, don't forget that many things can upset

146

the regularity of menstruation. Anything that can upset your neurohormonal system such as emotional and nutritional stresses can do it. So can the odors of women who live with you. Michael J. Russell of Sonoma State Hospital in Eldridge, California found that perspiration from a female donor, applied to the upper lip of other women (in an ethanol solution), brought the menstrual cycles of these other women into synchrony with the cycle of the donor. It is surprising that as many women are as regular as the statistics seem to say they are.

Let's look now at some of the remaining steps in the female sexual cycle and how the moon can influence them.

Ovulation and Conception

While it is an easy matter to identify the onset of menstruation, it is not so easy to determine when an egg is released at ovulation. Opinions have differed widely. But now there is a growing agreement that ovulation occurs about halfway through the monthly menstrual cycle. That agreement is based on observations and measurements of things such as body temperature and heart rate, which undergo specific changes when an egg is released from the ovaries.

Recent findings confirm those earlier observations. There is a gradual increase in the body's electrical voltages as ovulation is approached, with an abrupt peak when the follicle ruptures to release its egg. Some women have more than one peak a month, some have none, and some have their peak at any time during the month. But most women have one peak, on the day they ovulate, about midway through their menstrual cycle. These peaks are largest when there is a Full Moon. And perhaps there may be a force that stimulates the release of eggs during the Full Moon, more often than at other times of the month.

Human egg cells are about as big as a grain of refined salt. It would take the monthly output of 2 million women to fill a thimble with egg cells. And they are short-lived. They must be fertilized within two or three days or

147

they will be discharged with the next menstrual cycle. Yet there is only one chance in about 70 million that a sperm cell will reach the egg cell during each attempt. Therefore, a man who produces less than 70 million spermatozoa during a discharge is not likely to become a father. A highly virile man will release about 185 million sperm cells during a single attempt. Between these two extremes, you can see that it takes about 100 million sperm to fertilize one egg!

These 100 million sperm then enter a race to see who will get to the egg first. Sperm wiggle along at about one-eighth of an inch a minute. It's the same speed whether it is rabbit sperm, bull sperm or human sperm. At that rate, the sperm will have reached the female egg in about an hour from the time of entry in the race. And the winner will be the only sperm cell to fertilize the egg. That's because the first sperm to reach the egg triggers it into immediate action to block further penetration by other sperm.

It "blocks" in several steps. First, there is the "fast block." As the first sperm penetrates the egg surface, it causes the voltage across that surface to change from negative to positive. (The inside of the cell starts out being negative with respect to the outside, but then reverses.) That voltage isn't very high. It would take the voltages of tens of thousands of egg cells to add up to one volt. One dry cell for your battery is 1½ volts. Once the "fast block" voltage is established, it keeps other sperm from entering for several minutes. By that time, the "slow block" will take over. That consists of changes in the outer layers of the egg cell that produce sperm-killing chemicals, and more permanent structural changes which eliminate the sites to which sperm cells can usually attach themselves.

Notice that fertilization depends on the electric fields at the surface of the egg cells. Anything which can affect those fields would affect the likelihood of sperm penetration and the process of conception. We do know that the changing phases of the moon produce overall changes in the electrical voltages measured on the bodies of women. And we do know that births, which occur exactly nine

148

, lunar months after conception, follow patterns related to the phases of the moon.

But not all conceptions will occur under a Full Moon. Indeed, there seems to be evidence that a woman will be more likely to conceive, and to give birth, under a phase of the moon which is the same as her own natal moon phase.

That was one of the findings of Dr. Eugen Jonas, the Director of the Psychiatric Department of one of the State Clinics in Czechoslovakia. Those findings have led to his becoming known as the father of "astrological birth control." Briefly, he found that there is an optimum time of the month in which a woman can conceive a child. That time is when the moon is in the same position with respect to the sun as it was during the day she was born. In other words, you are more likely to conceive a child during your natal moon phase!

Jonas also claims that you can have a boy or a girl, depending on the sign of the moon. The signs are alternately male and female, as you go through the zodiac, starting with Aries as male. A conception in the moon sign of Taurus should produce a girl, in Gemini a boy, and so on. All you have to do is find the upcoming dates for the moon phases that are the same as your natal moon phase. Then you would find the moon signs for those dates. You would then select the time for your conception from the dates on which your moon sign sex preference coincides with the date of your natal moon phase.

It's only natural to wonder how the moon sign can have anything to do with the sex of a child that is about to be conceived. There are several possibilities. First, you must recognize that the sex of a child depends on the "sex" of the sperm cell that fertilized the egg. If a female sperm cell fertilized the egg, then it will grow into a girl. If it is a male sperm, it will become a boy. It's a race between the sperm cells. But it's not a fair race. It all depends on the conditions of the "track."

Male and female sperm cells carry different handicaps at different times. It has to do with the acidity or alkalinity of the "track" from vagina to uterus. If the track is acidic, female sperm have a better chance. If it is alkaline, male sperm are the favorites. It also has to do with whether the sperm get there before the egg and have to wait there until an egg arrives. Male sperm die sooner than female sperm. Therefore, if ovulation occurs too long after intercourse, say over 24 hours, the male sperm are more likely to have died by the time the egg arrives. The surviving larger number of female sperm would then be there to meet, and fertilize, the egg.

You can see then that the sex of a child depends on how the male and female sperm are handicapped in their race to be first to fertilize the egg. In one case it is the chemistry of the track. Acid favors girls and alkaline favors boys. (Now I know why my father-in-law always said to drink tomato juice to have a little girl.) In the other case, the sex of the child has to do with the timing between intercourse and ovulation. Intercourse before ovulation favors girls. Intercourse near ovulation favors boys, especially since the cervical fluids are especially alkaline at that time.

But there are other ways that semen can be separated into male and female sperm. In animal husbandry there are requirements for male or female offspring, depending on the needs. Artificial insemination techniques have been developed to meet those needs. In one technique, a weak electric field is applied to the semen to separate it into male and female sperm. These are then used to obtain the desired sex of the offspring.

Other techniques include the use of centrifugal forces that mimic gravity in the attempt to separate sperm according to their different weights. The success of this method means that male and female sperm, having different weights, are susceptible to separation by gravitational forces.

Perhaps the moon's influence on the determination of the sex of a child depends on its role in affecting the gravitational and electrical fields which in turn serve to separate semen into male and female sperm. As you know by now, moon signs indicate the status of those patterns of gravitational and electric fields. Jonas knew about these claims for the moon's influence over the female reproductive functions when he set out to "rediscover" them. And

150

so again, old truths are seen in a new light. That goes for the old truths about the time of birth as well.

Giving Birth

There have been many midwives' tales about when to expect the birth of a child. Most have been smiled at. But today there is no question about the fact that the number of births varies in periodic patterns. These include daily, weekly, monthly and annual patterns of increasing and then decreasing numbers of births. There is an early morning peak which has been "rediscovered" several times over the past century or so. That cycle is related to the daily changes in glandular secretions and the way they are metabolized.

Over 60 percent of births start in the early morning hours, soon after midnight. The remaining 40 percent begin during the day, with a marked minimum around midday. However, it has been found that disturbances in geomagnetic activities have also disturbed that hourly pattern of births. It may be that the dawn-to-dusk fields set up by our solar wind also set up the forces that induce labor, depending on how close the fetus is to its delivery time. Those fields would of course be affected by geomagnetic disturbances, as well as by the changing phases of the moon.

And indeed, such links between birthrates and moon phases have been found. There is a peak in the birthrate at around the Full Moon, and a minimum around the New Moon. The birthrate begins to rise rapidly from day 12 to day 14, and then drops sharply from day 15 to day 16. Studies which lump data on both sides of a Full Moon would of course find little change at the Full Moon since they average the pre-Full Moon peak with the post-Full Moon drop. Most studies of birthrates are troubled by such problems of grouping of the data.

Such statistics do not mean that you should expect your child to be delivered by the light of the Full Moon. Remember, Dr. Jonas' theory says that you will probably conceive and deliver your child during the moon phase that corresponds with your natal moon phase.

In addition to these hourly and monthly regularities in the number of births, there are weekly and yearly regularities. For example, there are preferred days of the week when more babies are born than on other days. However, the statistical data here seem to depend on the geographical locations, and the social preferences in those areas. In some places there is a maximum on Wednesday, with a minimum on Monday, and "never on Sunday." That's in Prague. Perhaps in America it would be "never on Wednesday," since the data do seem to show something about the preferences of doctors and mothers. Data from private hospitals show decided peak days of preference, while general hospitals are more evenly distributed across the week.

Annual peaks in the numbers of births occur during August and September. The timing of those peaks seems to be undergoing longer-term drifts which may be related to an interaction between solar events and lunar orbital cycles in multiples of nine years. But few people would find it useful to base their sexual activities or planned parenthood on such longer-term cycles. For that, they are best advised to keep an eye on that master clock of sexual functions, the 29.5-day synodic lunar month.

Let's see what you can learn from your lunar month about what mood swings to expect, and why you can expect them.

Your Lunar Sex Cycle

When you look at all the evidence, it seems pretty certain that your reproductive cycle is based on the synodic month that measures the time from one New Moon to the next. The data suggests that, once upon a time, women menstruated at the New Moon and ovulated a half cycle later at the Full Moon. Since conception must occur close to the time of ovulation, children were conceived under a Full Moon, and born, nine synodic months later, under a Full Moon.

As time went on, this pattern of menstruation, ovulation, conception and delivery must have slipped in its dependency on specific moon triggers. However, those sexual functions maintained their lunar periodicities

152

through the mechanism of imprinting. The day of birth is imprinted as though it were a day of the Full Moon. That imprinting then sets up an internal calendar that tells you when to menstruate, when to ovulate and when to give birth. And how to feel about things during those important periods of time. It sets the mood for love, and for withdrawal. It encourages those sexy feelings when such feelings are most likely to climax in a conception.

Women do not need to consult the results of scientific studies to know that there is a relationship between their feelings and their menstrual cycles. For example, it does not surprise women that studies have confirmed that fatigue and depression are greatest during menstruation. They also know from experience that they undergo outbursts of physical and mental activity before the onset of their periods. And that these times are noted for their feelings of high tension and irritability.

However, women may be less aware of the periodic increases in their feelings of sexuality and elation which follow menstruation. Those feelings peak even higher at the time of ovulation. Dr. Jonas found in his patients such peaks of sexual feelings when the moon was in the same phase as the natal moon phase. It seems reasonable that sexual feelings would rise as ovulation takes place. That would be nature's way to assure the reproduction of the species. Aside from its reasonableness, the evidence shows that there is a peak in the number of sexual encounters of women during the middle of their menstrual cycles. Further, there is a peak in the number of orgasms during the mid-cycle.

Of course there is a negative side of the coin. It is well established that both violent crimes and suicides vary in incidence among women in relation to the menstrual cycle. To the extent that these feelings would be more likely during the menstrual half of the cycle, rather than the ovulation half, you should be alert to them at the phase of the moon opposite your natal moon phase. Forewarned, forearmed!

One of the many interesting things that you can do with the tables and charts in Chapter 4 is to find the pattern of moon phases and signs that accompany your sex-related feelings and functions. Once you learn how those feelings show up in terms of moon phases versus natal phases, you can then use the tables to predict the dates of those upcoming conditions that can be so important in your life.

Let's move on now to see what the astrologers have to say about you, based on your time of birth.

8
The Moon and Astrology

Introduction

It's been said that the Romans set up the twelve-person jury system so that a defendant could be judged by persons from each of the twelve signs of the zodiac. This arrangement reflects the ancient astrological belief that the personalities and outlooks of people will be different, depending on the dates of their births. In fairness to the defendant, a jury should reflect all those outlooks.

Astrology is the study of how the changing positions of celestial objects can affect your character and your approach to daily life. It takes into account the relative positions between the planets, as seen from the earth at the time of birth. This includes the position of the moon. These birth, or natal, conditions are plotted on a chart called a horoscope. The resulting pattern of planetary positions is then used as a basis for the interpretation of the person's traits. It can also be used as a reference plot against which to compare the changing positions of the planets to see how they introduce changing influences into your life.

A complete natal horoscope takes into account all of the celestial objects of our solar system. Their positions are calculated for the precise moment of birth, as seen from the specific coordinates of a birth location. However, professional astrologers agree that considerable insight can be gained from your natal sun sign and moon sign, especially when both are examined together.

Your sun sign is considered to be a reflection of your conscious approach to life. Each of the signs of the zodiac is associated with specific traits which characterize the different approaches to life. Your moon sign, on the other hand, is considered to be a reflection of the traits which dominate your unconscious drives for expression. The signs signify the same traits for either the sun or the moon. The difference is in how those traits are expressed in your behavior. Most people will recognize their sun sign traits in their behavior. However, they may be unaware of their moon sign traits which only show themselves during impulsive responses, or as unfulfilled urges and desires.

One way you might check this out is to see how well your natal signs can describe you. You can also see if your friends and business associates fit these descriptions if you have their birthdates. First, you must find your sun sign, moon sign and moon phase from the tables in Chapter 4. Then you can use the listings in the following pages to see what the astrologers have to say about you, based on those natal conditions.

The first listing shows you the basic traits that are attributed to each of the signs of the zodiac. Remember, these are your conscious traits for your sun sign, and your unconscious traits for your moon sign.

The second listing is for your natal moon phase. You recall that the moon's phase tells you the relationship between the sun sign and the moon sign. Astrological significance is attributed to these different relationships which are revealed by the natal moon phase.

The third and longest listing is for the combination of specific sun signs and moon signs. Here you can see what the astrologers have to say about the specific combination of your sun sign and moon sign.

156

Traits of the Signs

The customary way in which the signs of the zodiac are characterized is by a list of terms which best describe the traits that are associated with those signs. The following list is typical of the terms used to characterize each of the twelve signs.

Aries—Creative, impulsive, ambitious, competitive, courageous, self-starting, confident, blunt.

Taurus—Productive, unhurried, resourceful, patient, steadfast (or stubborn), affectionate, stable.

Gemini—Intelligent, communicative, adaptable, social, versatile, excitable, curious, quick, diversified.

Cancer—Domestically inclined, emotionally sensitive, tenacious, cautious, insecure, loner, tireless.

Leo—Energetic, confident, generous, affectionate, loyal, forgiving, trusting, dignified, authoritative.

Virgo—Perfectionist, hard worker, competent, discriminating, communicative, methodical, modest, tactful, reliable.

Libra—Sympathetic, considerate, gentle, communicative, orderly, artistic, fair, affectionate, tactful.

Scorpio—Passionate, strong-willed, incisive, silent, forceful, sensitive, exacting, perceptive, intense.

Sagittarius—Idealistic, enthusiastic, intuitive, bright, proud, philosophical, athletic, communicative, fair.

Capricorn—Ambitious, persistent, methodical, cautious, moral, reliable, organized; possesses integrity, initiative.

Aquarius—Cooperative, independent, creative, impersonal, moderate, noble, helpful, tolerant, respectful.

Pisces—Sensitive, artistic, impressionable, compassionate, impractical, aware, imaginative, indecisive, intuitive.

As you begin comparing your own, and other, sun signs and moon signs against this list, you will soon notice a pattern of "hits" which exceed the number that you would expect from pure chance. Those hits reflect the accumulated experience of centuries of observations.

You may also use this listing of traits of the signs to

157

get an additional insight into yourself. Astrologers believe that you are strongly influenced by the sign of the zodiac which appears just on the horizon at the moment of your birth. That sign is called your Ascendant. You can find your Ascendant from your natal moon sign. I show you how to do that in Chapter 9. Once you find your Ascendant, you can check the traits of that sign to get a deeper insight into your temperament, or the basic grain of your character.

Interpreting Your Natal Moon Phase

Your natal moon phase, which shows the relation between your sun sign and your moon sign, reflects the difference between the sun season and moon season environments at the time of your birth. Astrologers have found that this has a bearing on the way your conscious (solar) and unconscious (lunar) traits interact with each other. That in turn determines how you approach your relationships with other people. You may be well aware of your conscious traits, but your behavior with other people depends on how those conscious traits are amplified or offset by your unconscious traits.

After you find your natal moon phase, in days of the moon's age (in Chapter 4), check it against the following list of astrological interpretations to see how well you fit into the eight general patterns.

New Moon to Waxing Crescent (0 to 3 days)

You approach your relationships with an impulsive emotional response. Your instincts and intuitions are sharply tuned to all the things that go on around you. However, you see these things subjectively, in terms of what they mean to you, rather than for what they might seem to be to an objective observer. Although you really do know what your impressions are telling you, you persist in projecting yourself onto others and trying to force life and love to conform to your favorite dreams.

Waxing Crescent to First Quarter (4 to 7 days)

Your need is for new challenges. You seek them out with an eagerness that often seems like impulsiveness. You try to bring interesting changes into your relationships as a means for expressing your creative impulses and as a way of asserting your self-confidence. However, in spite of that confidence in yourself, you are an easy victim to a preoccupation with the past. You must learn to accept that "what is done, is done!"

First Quarter to Waxing Gibbous (8 to 11 days)

You are the strong-willed manager who is impatient with the failures of the past. You can't wait to rebuild the world into the future that you know it can become. Your sense of urgency in trying to bring about the needed changes can make you seem ruthless. Yet, in spite of that urgency, you take the time to plan and to work hard for the changes that you feel are so necessary. Fortunately, you can recognize and cope with the crises that you often create in your zealous approach to life.

Waxing Gibbous to Full Moon (12 to 15 days)

No one can put anything over on you. You are much too aware of what's going on! And when you don't know what's going on, you make it your business to find out, fast. You have a need to contribute your perceptive skills to the clarification of causes or social issues. Once you do so, you can devote yourself to its full support. Or to the support of a leading personality who carries the banner for that cause. You also expect others to support you with that same devotion. Most of the time you are trying to answer your own most frequently asked question, "Why?"

Full Moon to Waning Gibbous (16 to 18 days)

Your relationships with others are very important to you. And yet you approach those relationships as though

159

from a great distance. That's because you have to see how the whole world fits into the picture. Everyone has to be in their proper places, and play their proper roles. You tend to think of things in absolutes, with little patience for their subjective aspects. This makes you come off as a perfectionist. Unless you learn to compensate for this by considering the emotional side of things, you will be pulled apart by trying to live in a world of conflicting absolutes.

Waning Gibbous to Last Quarter (19 to 22 days)

Your need is to share all your knowledge and all your experiences with others. You enjoy learning new things, and doing new things. That's so you can then explain them, or show others how to do them. You are always on the lookout for new things from diverse areas of interest. And then you try to pull all those things into an integrated picture, so that you can show all your friends what you have discovered. You are a disseminator of ideas, a popularizer. You can easily become a crusader for a cause. You have to guard against becoming over-enthusiastic lest you slip into fanaticism.

Last Quarter to Waning Crescent (23 to 26 days)

Your relationships with others are marked by your need to force issues based on what you consider to be "principles" that must be upheld. You have the ability to sense future crises before others become aware of them. And you are impatient with those who refuse to make the changes that you believe are necessary to resolve those crises. Your lack of flexibility in trying to convince others leads them to reject your efforts. You then take comfort in believing that posterity will prove you were right after all. You should try to develop a sense of humor, or the ability to back off, to avoid the pain you feel when others criticize your views.

Waxing Crescent to New Moon (27 to 0 days)

You approach a new relationship with your eye on where it can lead to in the future. You have a prophetic

160

sense of future events, and you see all present activities as the seeds of those future events. If a relationship offers the promise of a future reward, you are quite willing to make the necessary sacrifices to assure receiving that reward. In a sense you feel that most of your relationships have been destined and would have come about one way or another. That fatalistic feeling can lead you into accepting hardships or difficult tasks as unavoidable. Unchecked, your fatalism can also lead to fanaticism. Keep balanced!

The Sun Sign and Moon Sign Combinations

The natal moon phase tells how far apart the sun sign and moon sign are from each other. But it doesn't tell which sun sign is how far away from which moon sign. The same moon phase can hold between twelve different pairs of signs. There are 144 specific combinations between the twelve sun signs and the twelve moon signs. And there is an astrological interpretation for each of these 144 pairs. These interpretations depend on how the conscious traits of the sun signs interact with the unconscious traits of the moon signs to produce an overall behavior pattern. The following listing of sun sign and moon sign pairs shows you the behavior patterns that astrologers have found to correspond with those pairs. Again, you can check this out by seeing how closely you are described by your sun sign and moon sign pair. Then check your friends.

Find your sun signs and moon signs from the tables in Chapter 4. Look for your sun sign first, and find your moon sign listed along that sun sign.

Sun in Aries—Moon in Aries

You have to turn everything into a contest so that you can pour your energies into the game of winning, whether at work or in the bedroom. You thrive on competition and impossible schedules. In spite of your rush through life, people find you charming. But they often wonder why you don't take the time to listen to them.

161

Especially your lover. Take the time to become aware of the needs of others.

Sun in Aries—Moon in Taurus

You love the good things of life. And you have the ambition, patience and common sense to know how to go about getting them. Fortunately, your ambition is guided by the old-fashioned work ethic, so you are fair in your dealings with people. However, your stubbornness bothers them. They can't see why you aren't a little more flexible. Even your lover feels the same way. If you learned how to discuss your feelings you would have fewer outbursts of jealous rage. You would do very well in creative arts if you weren't so worried about money. As you already know, your strong suit is your gentle art of verbal persuasion.

Sun in Aries—Moon in Gemini

You are extremely independent. Everything about you seems to be fast and furious as you keep looking for more exciting ways to do things. You think and talk fast. You have an answer for everything. Even when nobody asks you. Some people find you pushy. That's because you were in the closet when they passed out "tact." Yet you are popular. People admire your self-confidence and the ease with which you can get the most difficult things done. You need a patient partner who is interested in listening to the nonstop flow of your ideas.

Sun in Aries—Moon in Cancer

You are always at odds with yourself. On the one hand you have a restless nature that wants to go out and conquer the world. But then again, you need the safety and security of a nice home, cushioned in a nice fat bank account. You must learn to stop berating yourself for not doing all those things that you are afraid to try. Instead, you should focus on all those accomplishments that you hardly take credit for. Once you find your mate, your

162

loyalty is boundless—even though it is sometimes restless.

Sun in Aries–Moon in Leo

Your self-confidence is well placed. You have the courage to do anything, and the energies and abilities to bring it off. People listen to you when you talk. That's because you always manage to place yourself on center stage. Luckily, you can offset your superior bearing with a sense of humor and a willingness to share things openly with almost anyone. In fact, you are too open. You believe that everyone is as honest as you are. You are very giving in your romantic relationships as long as you feel that you are still in charge.

Sun in Aries–Moon in Virgo

Caution is your watchword. Adventure may be fine for others, but you prefer difficult assignments that challenge your intellectual abilities. Your competency in handling them gives you a needed sense of security. You are thorough in your attention to details, and your analyses are seldom wrong. That causes you problems when you have to show others where they went wrong. The trouble is that you end up criticizing their work rather than explaining where they fell off the sled. Although you are affectionate, your reserve keeps you from showing it to your lover. Your relationship would improve if you released your affections and reserved your impulse to find fault.

Sun in Aries–Moon in Libra

If you had written the Declaration of Independence, you would have guaranteed that no law be passed to restrict the pursuit of happiness. For you, that means anything goes. And the way you try to live, it usually does. People are attracted to you because you pursue such a different approach to life. You are charming, even though you insist that everyone do things your way. The problem is that you keep changing your mind about which way

163

things should be done. That's because you are trying to avoid responsibilities, and because so few things seem to fill your need for excitement and change. You should take up a relaxation technique, such as meditation, to help you get over those awful mood swings.

Sun in Aries—Moon in Scorpio

It's no secret to your friends that you enjoy a good fight. You will fight with anyone who cares to disagree with you. When you win, you are on top of the world. When you lose, it's the pit. But with your energies, you are seldom in the pit. If properly directed, this impulsive need to win can lead you to the top of your field. You have a sharp mind, and the concentration to help you master any profession—if you had the patience to train for one. As a lover, you are intensely sensuous and passionate. However, your partner had better agree with you that your role is one of protector. Unfortunately, the relationship won't survive many disagreements.

Sun in Aries—Moon in Sagittarius

You really come on like a child discovering the mysteries of a beautiful world each day. Wide-eyed and eager, you see life as a continuous round of adventures. And there had better be more adventures coming up tomorrow, because you will quickly become bored with the last one. The greatest problem you have to face is finding that ideal dream project to work on for the rest of your life. Until you find it, you are in danger of drifting through life in search of a mission. Your openness and willingness to share everything makes you an easy target for exploitation. However, once you settle down, your enthusiasm flows freely into your work and your loved ones. And your life becomes a joy to live, and a joy to behold.

Sun in Aries—Moon in Capricorn

You make no effort to conceal your desire for power and the status that goes with it. That's because your ap-

164

proach to those goals is aboveboard and reflects your intention to work hard to attain them. Your calculating and methodical manner is offset by a personal charm which disarms those who might otherwise come to fear you. As it is, they respect your maturity, and your decisiveness in dealing with problems. You are quick to reward a friendship, and slow to forget an affront. Your love life is driven by this same need for power and recognition. Unfortunately, your relationships are often blocked by your own deep sense of insecurity.

Sun in Aries—Moon in Aquarius

You are so far ahead of everyone else that they can't seem to understand you. Your intuition shows you where to go, and your energy gets you there first. It doesn't take you long to figure out what has to be done. But you are blind to the inabilities of others to see it the same way that you see it. That makes you seem rigid and even arrogant. Especially since you are so quick to take offense, and so open in the display of your anger. Your need for freedom of action makes it harder for you to accept the restrictions of an involvement with an individual or a group. You would rather be a loner. Fortunately, you get your pleasure from being the first one to blaze a new trail.

Sun in Aries—Moon in Pisces

Poor thing. Such emotional turmoil. Pulled by your strong desire to express yourself, yet blocked by your fears and feelings of insecurity. You just can't seem to overcome those fears to step out and do your own thing. And you try so often. You are like a chameleon, taking on the feelings and expectations of those around you— just so they will approve of you. Your best bet is to be with those who love you, and who will encourage you to fulfill your own needs. Especially if they encourage you to pursue your artistic and creative impulses. You have to be careful to keep your feelings of insecurity from following you into the bedroom. Keep your mind focused on your good points. You have many.

165

Sun in Taurus—Moon in Aries

You do not have to read a book to learn how to take care of Number One. You could write your own book. Once you have your eye on something you want, it's a safe bet that you're going to get it. Thank goodness you have the sense to use caution when it comes down to eyeball to eyeball standoffs. And that you have learned how to be a diplomat when it comes to easing people out of your path. You can be powerfully persuasive. You also run your love life on a double standard. If you expect loyalty, you owe your partner the same loyalty. That would be one way to put an end to your jealous rages. Another would be to recognize that there are more important things in the world than being Number One.

Sun in Taurus—Moon in Taurus

Your outstanding quality, which shows up in everything you do, is your unpretentious self-assurance. Your friends think of you as the strong silent type. You are the patient, understanding listener who can see through all the confusions and then come up with a simple commonsense answer to the most perplexing problem. You have a wholesome approach to life, with a natural bent for staying close to the basics. This may make you seem to be somewhat conventional, especially to your lover. You might try something a little more daring and imaginative every now and then. You should also loosen up a bit in your rigid approach to other people. You are basically affectionate, and there's no reason you can't express those feelings more openly.

Sun in Taurus—Moon in Gemini

You are the first one to spot a problem, and usually the first one to tell everyone how it should be solved. That's because you are always out there, poking around for new and interesting things to keep you from being bored. And you get bored easily. Mysteries fascinate you. You can't resist playing detective. In fact, you approach

166

almost everything as if it were some sort of game. Your basic conflict is that you know you should take more time to finish what you are doing. But your interest is already caught up with something else that met your roving eye. The same problem comes up in your love life. You need more variety than most partners are willing to put up with. Fortunately for you, your charm and exciting ways keep your partners interested.

Sun in Taurus—Moon in Cancer

You wish you were as sure of yourself as others think you are. Your easy adaptability to the needs of others, or to the needs of circumstances, reflects your feelings of insecurity and the need for approval. Yet it's so easy for you to get that approval with your charm and easy manner. So why are you so easily hurt? And why do you brood over a minor hurt for so long? You should learn that it is not an aggressive act to tell others how you feel about something. In your love life, you need all the old romantic frills. You also need a loyal partner. Someone who can't stop telling you how wonderful you are. But then, you would have to avoid becoming so complacent that you crawl up into a safe shell, passing up opportunities for developing your artistic and creative impulses.

Sun in Taurus—Moon in Leo

You are onstage all the time. Furthermore, you become your own spotlight, showing the audience where to look and telling them when to applaud. And they do applaud, because you are really something to behold. Your performances are never dull. You always try to bring a little more happiness to those who are a little less fortunate. You usually size up a situation quickly, but then you hold onto that impression stubbornly. Your opinions are so rigid that you can't hear anyone else's views on the matter. Your love life is also governed by your need to dominate. Let up a little, and give your partner a chance once in awhile.

167

Sun in Taurus—Moon in Virgo

You find that most things come your way very easily. You always seem to know what's going on in the world around you, and everyone comes to you to find out. You are one of the rare people who can see the big picture while still being able to focus your attention on the minor details. You can come up with plans for anything. They may not be imaginative, but they will be practical and will work. In the affairs of love you are a dream partner. You are loving and dependable. Perhaps too dependable. Let yourself be carried away once in awhile.

Sun in Taurus—Moon in Libra

No one really knows how restless you are under that nice calm facade. You carry it off so well. People are attracted to your wise and worldly ways. And you keep them enchanted with your sensitive sympathy for their deep-felt needs. You treat everyone with the respect of an equal. It's unlike you to knowingly hurt anyone. And, if someone hurts you, you are quick to forgive and forget. If you had your way, you would flee from the hassles of life and take a job as a forest ranger. You can overcome that temptation by getting involved with more aggressive people. Your love life needs a sympathetic partner who can give you that delicate attention you crave.

Sun in Taurus—Moon in Scorpio

Don't take things so seriously! The world isn't really out to get you, no matter what you think you see going on all around you. Sure, the papers are filled with violence and corruption. But there are lots of nice things going on that don't make the papers. Life is a smorgasbord. That doesn't mean you have to walk down to the crummy side of the table to eat. There's roast beef at the other end. If you can get your fears off your chest, they might make room for other, more positive feelings. You have the willpower to do that if you really want to. You are an affectionate lover, but you tend to be overprotec-

168

tive. Also, try not to turn your love bed into a therapy couch.

Sun in Taurus—Moon in Sagittarius

You can see the future, and you know it can be yours. You have the faith and the practical skills to make your dreams come true—if it weren't for the fact that you are off on another dream before you bring the first one down to earth. You love the nice things in life. The expensive things. But you spend all your money so fast that you never have any left over to buy them. Some of that fast spending is wasted on impulsive generosity which you lavish on loved ones and friends. Your love life is just as lavish and varied. But, in the end, you are looking for that one true love to share your fantasy world with you.

Sun in Taurus—Moon in Capricorn

People love you for your gift of brightening up conversations with your wit and humor. Little do they know about the deep concerns feeding on your self-doubts. These doubts block your enthusiasm for trying to do anything "big." You feel, "Why try? I might lose everything I have." What a pity! Your fears are unfounded. You can really do the things you dream about. All it takes is for you to screw up your courage a notch or two. You won't let yourself down once you get started. You have a natural talent for getting things organized. You could easily become a wheeler-dealer. Better stick to your artistic talents. As a lover, you expect too much, and accept too little. That can change as soon as you build up your confidence.

Sun in Taurus—Moon in Aquarius

If there is such a thing as a realistic visionary, you would be the perfect example. Perhaps you do dream too much. But your patience and determination combine with your resourcefulness and creative insights to make many of your dreams come true. It's hard for you to form strong relationships because of your need for independence. Unfortunately, some people interpret that independence as a sign of aloofness. But that's before they come in contact with your eager kindness and responsiveness to the needs of others. Now, if you can only learn to control those unpredictable outbursts of anger, things will go more smoothly for you. Your love life is an example of an exercise in imagination, and a tolerance for novelty.

Sun in Taurus—Moon in Pisces

You move among your friends as though you are walking on eggs. You are so fearful of fracturing their fragile feelings. It's one thing to be compassionate, but aren't you carrying it a bit too far? Doesn't it make you feel self-conscious to be so worried all the time about how others will feel? Actually, those concerns are causing you to miss out on the great opportunities to learn from the everyday stress situations that come up between friends. You don't have to keep backing off from potential confrontations. You will feel better when you start expressing your own feelings and defending your own opinions. That goes for the bedroom too. Don't be such a pushover for your partner. Your rights are important too!

Sun in Gemini—Moon in Aries

You seem to be on a race through life. Slow down and enjoy the scenery. You keep going around the same laps over and over again without realizing it. No wonder you are getting bored. Slow down to see what's going on. Then maybe you won't have to be creating all that mischief just to liven things up. Your problem is that you are so busy telling everyone what you want that you can't hear what they want to bring to the party. You are like the bull that wants to rush up the hill to "kiss" a cow in the herd. If you walked up the hill instead, you would have the energy to "kiss them all." And with your sex drive, you would like that better anyway. It would be

170

nice if you learned to say thanks to the cow, after you "kissed" her.

Sun in Gemini–Moon in Taurus

You are like the lovable child who always means well but keeps making the same mistake over and over again. You never seem to learn, do you? You work so hard for a goal. And then when you get there, you need to try something else that's more exciting. Fortunately, you have the emotional stability to withstand the pressures of switching between your need for security and your need for adventure. You also have the kind of personality that always gets ahead in life. It is important that you maintain an active social life to give you the excitement that you can get only from having people around you. You also need an appreciative lover who isn't put off by your need for diversity.

Sun in Gemini–Moon in Gemini

You are like the person who leaped up on a horse and rode off in all directions at once. What seems to be a healthy vitality is really an outpouring of nervous energies. Not that you can't focus all that energy on a practical application, and do it efficiently at that. It's just that your interests are everywhere, and you follow those interests wherever they lead. There's no telling what kind of genius you could become if you ever focused on one thing. As it is, your genius is in getting around things, rather than dealing with them honestly. That comes easy for you since you seem to know what people are thinking about. Your love life is a string of love lives, each of which lasts too long as far as you are concerned.

Sun in Gemini–Moon in Cancer

You must feel that you were born on a roller coaster. Up and down, up and down. Those moods! Depression, elation, depression, elation. You become so involved in the feelings of others that you can't tell if you are depressed for yourself or for the person who just hung up

171

the phone. Also, you can't handle arguments at all. That's because you haven't learned that it's no sin to speak up for yourself. Once you recognize that your moods may be a reflection of the feelings of others, you will be able to shake them off and experience your own feelings more clearly. Then you can express them more accurately. As a lover, you recognize your own need for novelty, while still being responsive to the needs of your partner.

Sun in Gemini—Moon in Leo

You are the one who can sit down next to strangers and pour out your life story. And you do it so well that they will beg you to keep them posted on the next chapter. You take yourself more seriously than others think. They can't figure you out. Sometimes you seem so carefree and charming. But then you suddenly turn bossy, snapping out orders like a field commander. You know that you are playing a role to impress yourself with your own importance. But it sends the troops into hiding. You listen to the advice of others but end up doing things your own way. Your romantic needs are best met by someone who shares your desire for a comfortable family life, kids and all.

Sun in Gemini—Moon in Virgo

You have to talk to people, argue with them, teach them, share your views with them, anything as long as you can communicate. You must have an audience to charm, and to share in your latest findings. You're into everything, so you always have something to say to anyone you meet. Your problem is that you are into so many things. You expect too much of yourself in all of them. Since you can't do everything, you live in a fog of frustration. Give yourself a break. Be as compassionate toward yourself as you are toward others. Your love life is less than intense. That's because your mind is always somewhere else. Also, it would help if you were less critical of your partner.

172

Sun in Gemini—Moon in Libra

You're not happy until everyone around you is happy. So you keep yourself busy trying to resolve everyone's problems for them. You are good at it because of your tactful and sympathetic ways. Also, you happen to need all that involvement with other people to feel really alive. Unfortunately, you often end up feeling less happy than those you help. That's because you never take the time to develop or exploit your own talents, which are many. You could become interested in any one of many fields if you gave yourself the chance. Your romantic need for the ideal partner will take you through many partners before you settle down.

Sun in Gemini—Moon in Scorpio

You know exactly where you are going. And you're going to get there as carefully as possible. It's not important to you that anyone else should know what you are up to. In fact, you prefer that they don't know anything at all about you. You have the eye of a hawk when it comes to seeing what's going on around you. Your problem is that you then exaggerate what you see, just to make it seem more interesting or exciting. Although you are your own boss, you depend heavily on the ideas and approval of others. Once you make a decision, you defend it stubbornly. And you can overcome many setbacks to see it implemented. As a lover, you are always interested and always passionate. But your possessiveness takes you to the extreme of pointless jealousy.

Sun in Gemini—Moon in Sagittarius

It's a good thing that you have such a short memory. That way you can't remember how much you expected of yourself yesterday. And how little of it came to pass. Brilliant but naive. It's a new world to you every day. You can fashion enough dreams to keep a dozen people busy for the rest of their lives. Unfortunately, your impulsiveness, impatience and spendthrift ways keep you from

173

following up on even one of your brilliant visions, especially if it requires working out a few details. My, what you could do if you ever got organized! Your love life is equally hectic. Your double standard makes one wonder who said good-bye to whom in your revolving-door affairs.

Sun in Gemini—Moon in Capricorn

You know that you are going to be a success. And you know that people are going to help you achieve that success. The reason that you know all this is because that's the way you have it planned. You're pretty cool. And calculating. But not ruthless! Your sense of dignity and moral righteousness keeps you from resorting to unethical practices. You would rather not succeed if you have to lie and cheat. Your problem is that you deal with people as though they were pieces on a chessboard. In romance, you pick your partners for the prestige they can bring you. Even if you can't feel more than loyalty and devotion, try to show some affection occasionally.

Sun in Gemini—Moon in Aquarius

People have to restrain you from taking everything apart to see what makes it tick. You have a fascination for anything that's new and different. That's why you have so many of your own ideas for new ways to do old things. Your creative energies seem to be focused on the future. You're such an optimist that you can't understand all the gloom-and-doom stuff around you. The emotional problems of others confuse you. But you do whatever you can to be helpful. And your charm does seem to help. You need plenty of elbow room for yourself. Your love life is an endless search for that pedestaled partner. After you find one, you will have trouble accepting those tarnish spots that seem to emerge with the passage of time.

Sun in Gemini—Moon in Pisces

You would like to think of yourself as a cool, analytical, detached sophisticate. If only it wasn't for those nag-

174

ging feelings of compassion for others. They make you feel so emotionally vulnerable. Your efforts to repress those feelings can cause you to lose touch with them. Instead, you should accept them, and use them as guides that tell you how others are feeling. In fact, many of your feelings are intuitive perceptions of the feelings of those around you. You can put that to good use in your business. It also suggests that you keep your associations limited to those whose feelings you enjoy sharing. Your romantic nature is very attractive to the opposite sex. But you need a partner who is as sensitive and generous as you are.

Sun in Cancer—Moon in Aries

Inside you there is an impatient "doer" trying to break out through your shell of self-doubt. First you say you will, and then you won't. Caution keeps you in check. And after it does, you sink into one of those moods where all you can think about is "I should have!" Actually, you can't really do all the things you want to do. Nobody can. So stop picking on yourself. Start focusing on developing your talents and skills. But don't get too carried away by them. You have to overcome your impatience if you ever want to master them for professional use. Your love life is intense. But you need a partner who knows how to support your ego. You can't carry that load alone.

Sun in Cancer—Moon in Taurus

To others, you may seem to be humble. But you know that it's just a cover for your shrewd confidence. That's your disguise to keep people from taking advantage of you, as they so often try to do. But you have learned how to see through most of them by now. Your school of hard knocks has taught you to ignore what people say, so you can live your own life, your own way. The problem is, you also cut yourself off from important emotional ties with others. You lose your temper too easily when you feel threatened. To you, a comment or a criticism is a threat. You love life is filled with restraint. You

175

find it hard to accept the sincerity of your lovers. But you enjoy yourself anyway.

Sun in Cancer—Moon in Gemini

It's not that you want to be known as a critic. It's just that with your memory for detail, your perception of fine nuances and your sophisticated wit, it's hard for you to restrain yourself from making all those penetrating remarks. You also have a problem in sorting out your conflicting impressions and feelings. You can't decide which are your own, and which belong to others. This prevents you from discovering what you really want for yourself. Once you learn how to recognize your own needs, and trust your feelings about them, you will be well on your way toward solving most of your problems. Your love partner should be someone who can cope with your excessive demands. But without dominating you.

Sun in Cancer—Moon in Cancer

You are so busy protecting yourself from everyone and everything that you often forget what it is that you are trying to protect. Your talents and abilities go unused as you spend most of your time building bigger barriers to hide behind. What are you so afraid of? Most people couldn't care less about what you are so interested in protecting. You would be excellent in a financial career. Spiritual things also fascinate you. If you follow a spiritual movement, beware of surrendering to the "safety" of a bizzare cult. Your love affairs are not easy for you. That's because you are afraid that by giving yourself to someone else, you leave yourself wide open. Especially to criticism.

Sun in Cancer—Moon in Leo

It must feel good to have all that talent, and the confidence to go with it. Especially when it's so important to you that everyone sees you as a success. So much so, that you can't even accept the best-intentioned criticism, much less the inevitable setbacks of any career. It's good that your successes arrive early in life, because it takes you so long to recover from a single setback. Your favorite reaction to a defeat is to strike the pose of the misunderstood martyr. Your love life is great when things are going well. But you fall out of bed the minute there is a problem anywhere in your life.

Sun in Cancer—Moon in Virgo

The reason that you grew up so much sooner than all your friends is that you caught on that much sooner that it is a hard, hard world out there. Your emotional sensitivity and intellectual perceptions brought you that news very early in life. But instead of letting it get you down, somehow you learned to accept the realities and to cope with them. In the face of an indifferent world, you are still up front with your kindness, generosity and understanding for anyone who needs it. You're always the first to volunteer for a worthy cause. It would be nice if you now learned to be as generous to yourself as you are to others. Your love life pleases you only when you feel that you are giving more than you are getting.

Sun in Cancer—Moon in Libra

You are so anxious to please everyone else that you have probably forgotten what it is that would please you. Worse yet, you are beginning to think that it's all a waste of time since you can't seem to please anyone anyway. So you are busy building a safe shell to hide in. Stop. A better strategy is for you to get involved with the kind of people that you think you would like to be like. You will soon be pleasing them, and pleasing yourself at the same time. Sure it's a risk. But the risk is worth it. It's nice to have the romantic expectations you have for your love life. And you're right, sex isn't everything. That's why you get more out of love than a physical experience.

Sun in Cancer—Moon in Scorpio

It's a waste of time for you to pretend modesty or humility. "Winner" is written all over you. And people

177

don't resent you when you do win. They expect it. You are the self-assured, quiet one. People believe that you have a mind like a computer. Little do they know that you decide everything from the bottom of your gut. And you trust yourself. You could improve your public image if you weren't so quick to point out other people's faults. And so slow to forgive the people who point out your faults. You would be less depressed, less often, if you were less secretive about your feelings. Especially those deep hurts. Your love life is vigorous and sensual. Yet, you are compassionate and protective. Don't smother your lover.

Sun in Cancer—Moon in Sagittarius

People enjoy being with you because you are always in such a good mood. Perhaps that's because your mind is always busy working away on another of your ambitious projects. You have many. If only you would get going on one of them. The reason you don't is that it's a hassle for you to choose between the "safe and sound" or the "wild blue yonder" project, so you go back to the drawing board for another inspiration. When you do settle down it will be in a conventional position that offers the security you need. That won't stifle you because you have your own way of giving wings to your soul. Your love life is like the rest of your life. You need variety, but have trouble deciding on who to settle down with. But you will be loyal.

Sun in Cancer—Moon in Capricorn

Few people suspect that you really are an ambitious person, under all those shy mannerisms of yours. Even you don't recognize your own drive for success. That's because you are torn between living in a risk-free comfortable cave and taking on the challenges of the rat race. The chances are that you are reading this from your comfortable cave. It doesn't have to be that way unless you really want it. Just follow your intuition. Your basic talent for organization, along with your keen perception, are excellent business skills. Your love life gives you more problems than pleasures. You want a warm relationship without being tied down. That hot-cold switch can turn off the most understanding lover.

Sun in Cancer—Moon in Aquarius

You are the kind of person who opened up the West. And, going back further, like the ones who tossed tea overboard at the Boston Tea Party. You're always ahead of everyone else in breaking down old ways, or opening up new ones. Your problem is that you're indifferent to anyone else's ideas as you forge full steam ahead on your own. That can be a problem when you find yourself out there, all alone, caught between your visions and your insecurities. You could become a cynic. Or, you could run for the protection of a cult that dishes out its own version of cloud-nine visions. Your love life is based as much on friendship as it is on romance. But your partner will have to learn to cope with your moodiness and irritability.

Sun in Cancer—Moon in Pisces

You are the first person your friends come to when they have a problem. Your compassion and generosity reach out to people even before they have to ask for it. You really can sense the needs of others. Fortunately, you don't allow yourself to get caught up in their problems. You keep a safe distance by play-acting out a helpful role, rather than by living it out. You can act tough, or fragile, depending on what the scene calls for. Your problem is that these roles become so much a part of your act that you forget that that's what they are. You should try to be yourself every so often, just to keep in touch with yourself. Your love life needs emotional support more than physical experiences. If you are betrayed by your lover, you may become severely depressed.

Sun in Leo—Moon in Aries

There's no way you could be lost in a crowd. You are the one everyone would spot immediately as "The

179

Boss." You are not afraid to speak your mind or do whatever comes into your mind. It makes little difference who stands up to you. You move right over them. And you love it. It's a good thing that you don't believe in hitting below the belt. Nor do you ever turn against a friendship. Your problem is that you make snap decisions before you give yourself a chance to get a better picture of what's going on. Try listening to those you trust. Your love life is a conflict between your loyalty to one and your need for adventure. Your best chance is for you to find a lover like yourself.

Sun in Leo—Moon in Taurus

You are a pillar of strength and wisdom—that is, when all is going well. Comes trouble, and you quickly fall apart. That's because you are too intense in what you expect of yourself. You have an intense need for the comforts of life. And you think that the only way to get them is by gaining power and status. Your dreams of luxuries are the fuel of your ambitions. Your problem is that you're so sure of your own judgment that you are blind to everyone else's opinions. You would do better if you learned to respect the opinions of others. Maybe then you would have fewer setbacks, and fewer of those depressions that go with them. You approach your sex life like you would a lusty meal. But you need a few lessons in your "table manners."

Sun in Leo—Moon in Gemini

You would do almost anything to be sure that you attract attention. Even if it comes down to insulting your friends to do it. You hate work. In World War II you would have been called a goldbrick. Maybe you don't think that you are lazy. But that's not what people think when they end up doing your share of the work. You have Sergeant Bilko's flair for fast-talking con games. You could do very well in many varied professions. You just lack the patience to settle down long enough to work at it. Your need for diversity dilutes your discipline. It also dilutes your love life, which is reduced to a search for yet more novelty. You need mental as well as physical stimulation from your partner.

Sun in Leo—Moon in Cancer

It must be nice to feel so secure in yourself that you don't have to prove anything to anyone. You have compassion for others. And you have many creative talents. Now, if only you had the ambition to go out and do something with these talents. Your friends wonder why you willingly accept so much less than what you are actually worth. But that's the price you are ready to pay to avoid the hang-ups of running in the rat race. Your problem is that you can easily become smugly complacent. You seem to be too proud to learn news skills. You think that it is humbling to admit that you have to learn from someone else. Your love life starts out with a search for variety. But it soon settles down to a dependable one-on-one partnership.

Sun in Leo—Moon in Leo

Your favorite person is the one you see smiling back at you from your morning mirror. You can't get over how fantastic you are. You sit like a king at court, awaiting the homage of your vassals. You smile, first this way and then that way. It confuses you when your subjects seem to have missed the point of your royal favors. Perhaps that's because they have learned how fickle you are with your favors. Your dignity demands that you recover quickly from such unkind ingratitude. Your compulsion for the luxuries of life will often lead you through shady paths to get to them. You work hard enough, but you do know a few shortcuts. You need to feel independent, even in your love life. Your affairs are many and varied. Your motto: "Why limit my favors to only a few?"

Sun in Leo—Moon in Virgo

You would love to show everyone how easily you can conquer your enemies. If only you didn't have to face them in a fight. You are looking for the riskless challenge.

So, you dream up some challenges, and win your wars between your ears. Still, you do slay real dragons. But it's from behind the protective shield of someone else up front. You are a harsh judge of others, and you make no secret of those judgments. Why must others meet your own high standards? It's not fair to expect them to be as perfect as you are. Let up on them. And, while you're at it, let up on yourself a little too. Your love life is one long search for the perfect partner. There are always shortcomings when measured against your puritanical taboos.

Sun in Leo—Moon in Libra

You are at your very best when you are called upon to be the peacemaker in a raging conflict. Your charm is like the oil on the stormy seas. Your sunny disposition brings a calmness in which dissensions are quickly dispelled. But then, your naive solutions don't last too long, because people are never as trustworthy as you expect them to be. It's hard for you to impose yourself on others. You would hate being a boss. Nor can you make a clear decision. Everything has an extra "yeah but . . ." that has to be considered. It's important for you to be liked by everyone. When you feel rejected you become anxious, and pull into a shell. You are flirtatious in your love life. That's because you love the attention it gets you. At heart, you are looking for that one sweetheart to call your own.

Sun in Leo—Moon in Scorpio

Your friends don't kid around with you. They have learned how serious you are about everything. You have a Master Plan for your life. It's more like a Battle Plan, and you are always on the lookout for the enemy. You plan your fun as seriously as you plan your work. You are not likely to give anyone an opportunity to take advantage of what they may think to be your weakness. You're much too ambitious to expose yourself as a potential pushover. You are also too stubborn to yield to a compromise. That rigidity builds up stresses which then explode in front of your friends and family. Try letting off that steam more slowly. You lay down strict rules for your lover, to whom you are then loyal. It's your possessiveness that leads you into all those jealous rages.

Sun in Leo—Moon in Sagittarius

You are the perennial optimist; you probably whistle while you work. You are always recalling your last fun-filled adventure, or planning the next one. Life for you is a continuous round of planning or implementing exciting activities. These usually involve getting a lot of people together for a trip or getting involved in a social cause. You are a born leader. But you have to learn to control those impulsive distractions long enough to finish one thing before you start the next. You are up-front with everyone about your feelings. You probably never tell a lie. It's hard for you to take a backseat in anything you do. But learn to keep your pride in check. You are a generous lover. And a loyal one, with many partners. Variety is the spice of your life.

Sun in Leo—Moon in Capricorn

Hail to the King! You move through life with the feeling of power that only a king would dare to presume. You can easily intimidate people with your authoritative postures and your regal ways. These are not mistaken by anyone as mere poses. Everyone knows that you are serious about yourself and your abilities. You know you are a leader. And you keep reminding others, lest they forget. Your subordinates live in fear of your steady stare-downs. If they only knew how insecure you felt at those times! They can easily breach your defenses once they recognize your need for admiration. Your need for love is a need for sex—delivered to you daily, with a side dish of flattery to go with it.

Sun in Leo—Moon in Aquarius

You're so cool that butter wouldn't melt in your mouth. Even when you are in the rat race, you never no-

183

tice it. Yet, your ambitions are quietly looking for ways to express themselves. Once you set your sight on a goal, there's no stopping you from reaching it. Still, you follow a simple, unpretentious life. Your love for humanity leads you to extend your hand to anyone in need of help. At times you can become so detached from things that you seem to be absentminded. You want to be logical in your decisions. But you always end up by deciding on the basis of your gut feelings at the time. Pressure confuses you. You have to learn to take things one at a time. Your love life is spiced by variety. You don't find it to be any trouble in breaking off one relationship as you start the next one.

Sun in Leo—Moon in Pisces

You always intend to go to the next PTA or church meeting. But first you have to put up that shelf, or start the new curtains. You know that you should get more involved with community affairs. But there's always so much to do at home. It's a pity, since the community could really benefit from your calm reasoning and art of persuasion. However, you have to get yourself comfortable in your own castle before going out to fight for the charities. You often feel guilty because you can't live up to your own high standards, or because you find it so easy to manipulate people, and you enjoy it. You also suffer from imagined ills and threats to your well-being. Relax. Your love life includes too many people for any one of them to feel that they are the special one. That can leave you in the dark. And alone.

Sun in Virgo—Moon in Aries

No matter how often you run out to the end of the diving board, you never seem to have the nerve to jump off. You may imagine yourself the hero of a hundred scenarios. But it's another story when it comes down to playing out the scene. It's time you faced it. You need your security more than you need all the heroics. Still, there are plenty of safe scenes for getting your thrills from conventional activities. You have the discipline and

184

work habits that qualify you for exciting professions. But you will have to learn to be a little less touchy, and to put a cap on that quick temper of yours. That would also be of great help in your love life. As it is, your jealous rages are ridiculous. It takes more than your loyalty to a partner to make a partnership work. Try thoughtfulness.

Sun in Virgo—Moon in Taurus

It's easy to visualize you at the turn of the century, sitting on a swing on a front porch. You are a living example of the old-fashioned work ethic. Honest, patient and a font of free-flowing cracker barrel wisdom. You may want others to see you as a stern character, but your sotf heart gives you away. People often secretly wish that they could be more like you. Things usually go so smoothly for you that you can easily fall into the trap of complacency. It's hard for you to open up to modern life-styles. But it won't hurt you to take a few risks, now and then, to help develop yourself further. Try to meet people who might bring some novelty into your life. Your love life is built on the foundations of trust and dependability. So it's nothing less than a lifetime marriage for you.

Sun in Virgo—Moon in Gemini

Your friends will be the first to admit that you are indeed brilliant. And cool. Perhaps, even a bit aloof. Nothing seems to ruffle your feathers. You keep your emotions so well hidden that you sometimes lose sight of them yourself. That's your way of keeping from being hurt by others. It also keeps you from having those emotional experiences that life is all about. You set yourself impossible goals. And then you drive yourself relentlessly in an effort to beat them. Slow down! No one is chasing you. Also, don't be so quick to see the faults of others, much less tell them what you see. Learn to be more tolerant. As a lover, you need to have your intellect stimulated before the other stimulations can do anything for you. Stop being so picky or you won't find a partner interested in either kind of stimulation.

185

Sun in Virgo—Moon in Cancer

Those of your friends who really know you, and who care for you, go out of their way to treat you like a fragile flower. That's because you bruise so easily. The first sign of tension or conflict, and you run for the hills. Which, in your case, means withdrawal into isolated corners of your mind, safe behind your protective fantasies. Unfortunately, this tactic has produced a repertoire of imaginary fears as well. You have to face them for what they are—just products of your imagination. Trace them back and drop them. Try to become involved with people who have a bright outlook. You will soon be feeling the same way. Also, it won't hurt anyone if you assert yourself more often. Especially when it comes to matters of love. A partner can unintentionally dominate you because of your eagerness to please. Be generous, yes. But to you, too.

Sun in Virgo—Moon in Leo

You are the kid who earned all the gold stars for good conduct. You were born knowing how to be good. No one had to spank you. You would walk back two miles to return two cents of extra change. You still pick up the gum wrappers that others throw down. You are always doing the dishes. No wonder you are bewildered by the dishonesty and corruption all around us today. And still you volunteer for the worst jobs, without putting in for the overtime pay. It's hard for your friends to believe that you are as humble as you really are. Don't weaken, or you will slip into bitterness. It's useless to tell you to stand up for your rights. Your love life is marked by this same kind of open giving. At least you should choose a deserving partner.

Sun in Virgo—Moon in Virgo

You can spot a phony in a minute. Your perceptions are uncanny. You also have a mind like a steel trap. Between your penetrating perceptions and your analytical mind, you can hold people in awe of your

186

powers. Few people would care to argue with you once you state your position as clearly as you do. Your problem is that you are the first to notice your own faults, and you are the most critical of them. Get involved with others who need your help. You will soon see yourself as they see you. Not bad at all. You are open to others and know how to take their advice. But be sure that you make your own decisions. In love, you need a dependable partner. One who can give you emotional support while accepting your affection.

Sun in Virgo—Moon in Libra

With your knack for smoothing out sticky problems between people, you should be in the diplomatic corps. People can't resist your charm. They melt under your subtle persuasions. Your problem is that you identify so closely with everyone that you sympathize with both views. You also "pick up" on their aggressive feelings, which then disturb you. When that happens, you have to get away from everyone to regain your sense of balance. You can do that by getting down to basics. A quiet walk, a simple yoga breathing exercise, a meditation. Your need for beautiful things leads you to want a physically attractive partner. Your love life would benefit from a better balance of give and take. You give more than you take.

Sun in Virgo—Moon in Scorpio

Sometimes you fool even yourself with your cool and cunning intellect. But you can't keep secrets from yourself. You move from one passion to the next by gut feelings rather than by your cold logic. You are a methodical worker with clear goals that you are certain to attain. But you are always under the cloak of secrecy. Your feelings are barely visible to clue others in dealing with you. Smile now and then to let them know where you stand. Or yell if you have to. You should also try to develop interests outside your line of work. You can easily become a work addict. Although you stick to conventional jobs, you really would like to do more exciting things. It may help if you introduce some changes into

187

your daily routine. You are a jealous lover. You don't own your partner, even if you are married. Be less helpful with your helpful criticism.

Sun in Virgo—Moon in Sagittarius

You might really enjoy life if every little impulse for adventure didn't produce an equal and opposite feeling of guilt. This leaves you with dreaming about adventures as you knuckle down to the job at hand. You really want to be out on your own. Perhaps to own your own business. With your organizational abilities, and your enthusiasm for work, you could easily make a success of it. You become bored quickly if you feel confined by your job or your home life. The tonic is to get out into a more varied social life. When you do, try not to let everyone know how bright you are. Or how dull they are. Your love life is a search for stimulation. That doesn't mean that you can't be loyal to one partner, provided that partner shares your need for exciting things to do.

Sun in Virgo—Moon in Capricorn

The person who lives with you has to be a saint. You are tough. You have such a driving ambition that nothing else seems to matter to you. You have been at this since the cradle. Your goals are clear. You know that no one is going to help you get what you want. So you're going to do it with your own two hands! You don't want pity, and you have none for those who can't make it in the jungle out there. Yet, outside your job and your own home, you come on like a shy, gentle, considerate person. A fellow worker who met you at a party wouldn't recognize you. That is, unless something happened to trigger your temper. Your love life needs plenty of sex. But you resent the time it takes away from your work. You prefer a brainy partner in life. Someone who can be your best friend.

Sun in Virgo—Moon in Aquarius

You are not one to blow your own horn or steal the spotlight. Your mind is too busy finding fascinating new

188

worlds to explore. The unknown is a magnet that attracts your imagination and curiosity. And it's not just an idle curiosity. Your talent for discrimination and your love for detailed work will draw you into one of the exploratory sciences. You need to ask your "whys" in an orderly way. You look at everything as though through a microscope. Your friends feel that you see them as specimens for study. And you do! You are too interested in people in general to be involved with persons in particular. That's hard on a love partner, who never knows what direction you are coming from. They would be correct if they guessed it as "friendship." Nothing wrong with experimenting on friends.

Sun in Virgo—Moon in Pisces

You are the nice person that everyone likes to invite to their parties to give it a touch of class. You are refined, gentle, sensitive and soft-spoken. You ooze serenity. You don't have an aggressive bone in your body. When you see it in others, it makes you wince and turn away. You have dedicated yourself to your work, making few demands on yourself beyond assuring a comfortable life. Your problem is that you are letting your creative talents lie dormant. Try meeting with others who have similar talents, but who are busy developing them. You will soon be doing the same with your own. In love, you are too ready to give in to the demands of your partner. Try to save some of yourself for someone who isn't too selfish to appreciate it.

Sun in Libra—Moon in Aries

There's a troublemaker in every crowd. You're the one in yours. Let's just say that you have to get into mischief every so often to keep from getting bored. You are usually so dependable that it's hard to believe you can be such a devil. You're not. But after sitting around doing nothing, your restlessness gets the better of you. You will defend an opposite viewpoint or create a discussion out of a fabrication just to get the kicks that go with it. You would be better off channeling all that restless energy into something constructive. Unfortunately, you spend so much time in fantasy land that you wouldn't recognize something constructive if it were pointed out to you. Yours is a romantic soul. But you keep trying to focus your lover's feelings onto your needs. That's more likely to happen when you begin meeting his or her needs.

Sun in Libra—Moon in Taurus

You can be enchanting. You have such an even disposition. And you have such charming ways in dealing with everyone. No one is left out of range of your kindness. You probably don't feel as hurried as you seem to be. It's just that you feel so needed, in so many places, that you don't want to keep anyone waiting for you. You surround yourself with most of the comforts of life. Not too many things—but they have to be things of the highest quality. You have your ambitions but are reluctant to pursue them if you think that someone may feel hurt. Anyone. You also become involved with sentimental attachments that blur your judgments when it comes to dealing with your own emotions. You need a romantic love life. That's why you place your partner on a pedestal. Clay feet and all.

Sun in Libra—Moon in Gemini

You really dig deeply into things, don't you? With your penetrating intellect, and drive to understand, you can see answers where others haven't yet seen the questions! When you talk, others listen. Not just because of all the interesting things that you have to say, but because you speak so eloquently. Occasionally, you lose that calm, graceful manner of yours. That's when you find it necessary to cut someone down to size with your razor-sharp tongue. Fortunately, you know how to get out of trouble just as easily as you get into it. You are attracted to metaphysics and the occult. But you have the perception to separate things of the light from things of the darkness. You are a naive lover, led on by your romantic expectations. Your only hope is for a partner who is equally romantic and giving.

190

Sun in Libra—Moon in Cancer

Your motto has always been, "You can catch more flies with honey than you can with vinegar." The honey you use is your charm and honest sympathy for others. You can be shrewd if necessary. And your perceptions tell when it's necessary. But, more often, you just enjoy sharing your optimism and subtle humor with others. You are an excellent judge of people. And you use that skill in both your social and business life. You know exactly what roles to play for each occasion. And you play them well. So well that you often forget that you are playing a role. Especially if it's a role that keeps someone else happy. Learn to pull back now and then, to feel what it's like to be yourself again. You love to read and can easily get lost in the world of books. Don't. People need you, and you need them. You need love as much as you need air to breathe. Try to find a lover who is as sensitive and caring as you are.

Sun in Libra—Moon in Leo

You're so nice to have around the house. Or at work. Or anyplace. You brighten up the darkest corners. You can dispel someone's deepest depression. You believe so strongly in the basic goodness of things that any situation seems to improve with your mere presence. It makes little difference that you also happen to be in it for all the compliments that you can get. If you let your need for applause get out of hand, it can cost you points in your popularity rating. You make most of your decisions on the basis of your gut feelings, rather than by trying to think them out. But somehow Lady Luck always seems to be at your side. Don't worry, she always will be. Your love life depends on finding that ideal partner. You are more in love with love than with a lover. Try for something more realistic.

Sun in Libra—Moon in Virgo

You are the one they had in mind in the gag, "Ask him what time it is and he tells you how to make a

191

watch!" You probably know how to make a watch. But no one would ever know it unless they asked you. You want everyone to like you, so you don't push yourself on anyone. You are shy, and always feel so awkward. You have to guard against doing the things that others want of you, just so you can gain their approval. Your shyness also keeps you from getting into new fields where your talents could serve you so well. You love work and are methodical about getting everything done just right. You are too easily bothered by the tensions you feel around you. Try to learn some relaxation techniques. Your love life comes alive when there's as much head as heart in it. But you are held back by prudish inhibitions. You require a partner with your own brand of needs.

Sun in Libra—Moon in Libra

You are the neighborhood "people watcher." You are fascinated by the comings and goings of everyone. You learn everything you can about them, especially their private lives. You know what's cooking in every pot. Or what they had for leftovers last week. Nothing escapes your notice. And you love to share everything you know with everyone you know. That has caused more than one scandal in the neighborhood. So far you haven't been caught in any of those uproars. But your meddling must serve someone's need, or your friends wouldn't be so anxious to have you drop by. They like you best when you are in one of your "up" moods. Then you become a gusher of gossip about who is doing what to whom, and why. Your own love life wouldn't make the gossip columns. That's because you have a stable relationship, more filled with love than variety.

Sun in Libra—Moon in Scorpio

You take great pride on your objectivity and fairness in dealing with other people. Most of the time you feel at ease with yourself. But other times you can feel those inner drives of ambition and passion beginning to stir. Your style is usually calm and smooth. But if an opportunity presents itself to obtain a personal advantage for yourself,

192

you move in quickly. You need to be involved with many people, working toward a common goal. Your problem is that you can become blind to everyone's opinion except your own. Your incisiveness will often lead to your selection to a position of leadership. You take the responsibility of that position seriously. Your love life needs the stability of an understanding partner, someone with whom you can share intellectual as well as physical interests.

Sun in Libra—Moon in Sagittarius

You may have thought that they wrote the song "Don't Fence Me In," just for you. You don't want anyone telling you what to think or what to do. "Live and Let Live" is your motto. All your cards are on the table, and you always deal from the top of the deck. Honesty is your middle name. Unfortunately, you think that means you have to tell everyone what you think about them. But honesty is no excuse for tactlessness. Your own standards are so high that most people can't measure up to them. It bothers you that so many people are willing to settle for so little in life. You would like nothing better than to be able to lift humanity to a higher plane of living. However, your idea of a higher plane is what others call "fantasy." Your lover partner finds you to be generous and warmly loving. When your mind isn't off somewhere by itself.

Sun in Libra—Moon in Capricorn

More than anything else, you are driven by the desire to get ahead. You take everything seriously. It is important to you that you act properly with others. You enjoy people, and you can be very outgoing in your charming ways. You are always on the alert for some sign that people have recognized your importance. Your need for approval brings out your best efforts, or most unusual behavior. You have developed a keen insight into what makes people tick. You often use that insight to help you manipulate others in the effort to bolster your ego. In all fairness, you often manipulate them toward their own best interests as well. You would enjoy the game of politics. You need an attractive love partner for your ego.

It might make for a better relationship if you could try being more affectionate.

Sun in Libra—Moon in Aquarius

You have friends by the hundreds. In fact, you wouldn't be able to list them all if you tried. That's because you need that many people to keep you from falling into the dreaded pit of loneliness. You have developed the necessary skills to assure your popularity with almost anyone you might meet. Those who you don't get with your charm, you capture with your ever-active mind. You're fascinated by everyone and everything. Your problem is that you live so much for the needs of others that you seldom go into yourself to see which of your own needs are being overlooked and neglected. You might correct that once you realize that making yourself happy is another way of making others happy too. Your love life is enhanced by your need to bring joy to the world. Finding a perfect partner would give your life its reason for being.

Sun in Libra—Moon in Pisces

Your serenity hides a deep sensitivity to the feelings of others. It hurts you to see others suffer. You often make personal sacrifices just to help someone you care about. You are surprisingly naive about the harsh facts of a hostile world. But you have learned how to make the necessary compromises with the realities out there. Still, you compromise just a bit too much. You have intuitive insights into the moods of those around you. You must learn to close your window to those insights occasionally, so you can reestablish contact with your own feelings. You are an imaginative lover, and very sensual. You may have a problem giving all your attention to one partner, since sex gives you such an ego boost.

Sun in Scorpio—Moon in Aries

You have carefully chosen your goals. And just as carefully you make sure you reach them. Aggressive and

194

independent, your self-confidence carries you through any setback. Although you are a loner, you can be very warm and compassionate. You are caught between humanitarian impulses and the need for power and status. Your problem is that it is hard for you to compromise. Your fellow workers respect you, even when you act as though you are your own boss. They admire your intense convictions, but could do without your stubbornness. If you are forced to accept another opinion, you stalk off in anger. But you soon get over it. Your love life is marked by possessiveness and jealousy. You need sex, and plenty of it, as an outlet for your energies.

Sun in Scorpio—Moon in Taurus

You are everything that people expect of a leader. You are shrewd, authoritative, and can instill confidence in others. You can see the big picture, and describe it to those who have to fill in the details. You know what has to be done, and you know what it takes to get it done. You're able to crystallize reality out of dreams. Your calm businesslike manner is a cloak for all your secrets. No one ever really knows what you are up to. You recover from your setbacks quickly. Your problem is that you may develop stubborn streaks that make it even harder for your friends to penetrate your protective shield. Your sex life is a banquet of affairs. You shower your favorite-of-the-moment with kindness, affection and even "loyalty."

Sun in Scorpio—Moon in Gemini

If you're not a top-notch salesperson by now, you missed your calling. Your charm, exuberance and gifts of persuasion are irresistible. You have a sharp wit and you use it with telling effect. You give the impression of knowing more than you actually do. You also give the impression of being easily upset or excessively emotional. But most of the time you are acting the role that's called for in that scene. You are smart enough to get into intellectual pursuits. But you're not interested in scholarship. Pursuit of pleasure is more up your alley. Sensational sex comes before your interest in developing your hidden talents. To you, sex is your talent. It's easy for you to accept a lazy life. Your love life is run from an address book, to which you have already added extra pages. You need a partner who can tame your temper and move with your mood swings.

Sun in Scorpio—Moon in Cancer

True. You have more than your fair share of luck. But you would be a winner anyway. People admire your self-confidence and adaptability to any situation. You are naturally poised, charming and persuasive. Your friends hover near you, just to get within your aura. You could easily exploit such a loyal group of admirers. But instead, you would rather be alone. You relate to people out of a sense of service to them. And you play your role so well that your detachment is never detected. You also seem to handle your own problems very well. So well in fact that you have a tendency to become smug. You never have a problem finding someone who is interested in you. Your love life thrives on sex. But don't be so possessive.

Sun in Scorpio—Moon in Leo

You always seem to be at that junction between the High Road and the Low Road—trying to decide whether to feed the flesh or save the soul. If only you were a weak person it would be easy. But your strong will keeps you from turning to others for help in staying on the right path. You have probably convinced yourself by now that you can have the best of both worlds. And you do. Your problem is that you are so proud of pulling it off that you have to boast about it. By now your successful exploits on both roads are beginning to bore your listeners. If you happen to hit a pothole now and then, it can set you back into lapses of self-pity. But not for long. Your love life is rich with gratifying experiences, not the least of which is the pleasure you get from trying to make your partner over into your own image.

196

Sun in Scorpio—Moon in Virgo

Sooner or later, one of your friends is going to nickname you Charlie Chan or Columbo. Probably it will be Columbo. You have a lot in common with that unassuming, soft-spoken, lovable detective. Nothing gets by your sharp eye, or your sixth sense. You can tell that something is wrong before the first whiff of smoke. And it doesn't take much smoke for you to find the fire. Unfortunately, you are more interested in finding out who to blame than you are in putting out the fire. You set high standards for yourself, and you thrive on the work it takes to meet those standards. You especially enjoy things that challenge your intellect. But don't get lost in the library. You have to overcome many of your puritanical blocks to be able to express your strong sexual needs. A devoted and understanding partner will be necessary for that.

Sun in Scorpio—Moon in Libra

You are the one that people go to when they want help in settling a dispute with others. You have an instinct for finding a fair solution and the charm to convince others to accept that decision. If only you could feel that same confidence in your own decisions! You are so tuned-in to others that you sometimes become confused as to whose feelings you are reacting to. Take that as a signal to "close down" for a while, to give yourself a chance to be in touch with your own emotions. A change of surroundings, a visit to old friends, or to new acquaintances, will break the pattern. You trust people and are willing to accept their different beliefs. But beware of those beliefs which offer simple solutions requiring blind acceptance. Your love life needs to be based on the pillars of devotion and fidelity. In today's market, partners with such qualities are few and far between. Try to enjoy your long search.

Sun in Scorpio—Moon in Scorpio

Regardless of your height, you stand out in a crowded room. Your deliberate gestures and imposing presence announce that an extremely interesting person is at hand. You can sense the mood of a group and manipulate it to meet your needs of the moment. Unfortunately, your own mood swings between such extremes that you can become either depressingly morbid or explosively violent. You might be able to overcome that problem if you learned to be less secretive about your accumulation of phobias, like your fear of death. Learn to talk them out. Since your moods reflect the feelings of others, try to associate with people who have positive outlooks on life. You have a lustful sex drive. You keep looking for that partner who will let you mold him or her into your idea of a perfect mate. Back off a bit, now and then.

Sun in Scorpio—Moon in Sagittarius

Chances are pretty good that you are a leader in a new consciousness-raising group in your area. You probably started the local group. Your intuitive insights help you pick your way through the confusing alternatives offered as paths leading to the higher planes of life. Your warmth and compassion for others brings them to you in clusters. Each group comes with its slightly different need. Somehow you manage to serve them all. Their common element is the search for spiritual truth. That's not an easy search for you, because your open mind can accept seemingly diverse beliefs as equally true in their different ways. People who become dogmatic in your presence soon discover how blunt you can be in expressing disapproval. Your love life is fun-loving and adventurous. But you need that one true love to make it all meaningful for you.

Sun in Scorpio—Moon in Capricorn

You would have a hard time concealing the fact that you are driven by your ambitions. You want power and status to help you obtain the admiration and respect that you feel you deserve. You work hard and long. It is difficult for you to accept yourself in less than the top position. If you can't be the boss, you would rather be out on your own in a one-person shop. However, your ability to

198

manipulate people usually gets you into those powerful top positions. But after you make it to the top, you can't accept the sincerity of the nice things that are said of you. That's because of your deep-seated sense of insecurity. Learn to accept those compliments. You earned them. But take it a little easier on your subordinates. They didn't set the same high standards on themselves that you did. Your love life focuses on physical sex. That is, unless you slipped your sex energies into your career instead.

Sun in Scorpio—Moon in Aquarius

You have such a strong need to be surrounded by people that you have learned how to attract a following. First you attract their attention with your offbeat ways. Then you fascinate them with your fare of sophisticated food for thought. That usually comes from "far out," since you are well ahead of the times. You can dish up your own creative versions of science fiction, or invent utopias to be built by the next generation. In spite of the admiration of your disciples, you still feel detached. That's because you find it hard to make emotional ties. You should recognize that without those ties to the feelings of others, you are deprived of important opportunities to learn from "give and take." Your love life thrives on a partner who can come up to your need for an audience. Your interest is then measured by the level of the applause.

Sun in Scorpio—Moon in Pisces

You are probably the pillar of your church. You were born with the Ten Commandments etched into your brain. No one has to tell you "Thou shalt not . . ." You never do. Sometimes your antennae pick up so much of the negativities around you that you feel like running off to hide in a cave. However, you soon recover from the depression and come out to do all the things that you know have to be done. You can play whatever role is necessary for that. However, you should be careful not to become so involved with those roles that you forget who you really are. When you suddenly feel all caught up in

199

tensions, break away into another activity, or get into a different group. Preferably one that is more in tune with your inner needs. Your love life is a healthy balance of give and take. You are a romantic. You must have a loyal and considerate mate.

Sun in Sagittarius—Moon in Aries

You are the one at the company staff meeting who stands up to point out the shocking inadequacy of the last pay raise. If there is something on your mind, you see no reason to hide it. And with your childlike enthusiasm, everything is on your mind. You seem to enjoy saying something very profound, but in a way that's bound to shock people into attention. When a loud silence greets one of your remarks, you can usually quip your way out of the explosive situation. Thank goodness that you pick on only the big guys. But do you always have to do it in front of a gleeful audience? Your problem is that half the time you are trying to correct some fault, while the rest of the time you are on an ego trip. Your love partner needs a big ear and a matching smile of admiration for you. As a reward, you offer your ardent passion.

Sun in Sagittarius—Moon in Taurus

You would probably mail a big check to an unknown charity that solicited you by mail as "Resident." Let's face it, you really are a soft touch. Perhaps that's because you think that everyone is as honest as you are. Perhaps that's your "payment" to prevent you from ever being in need yourself. Security is on your mind all the time. Your need for security blocks you from taking even the smallest risk. It leads you into accepting the safest of conventional jobs. Still, you keep promising that once you save enough money, you will take that big step. How much will "enough" be? In all fairness to you, you do approach life with a positive and optimistic outlook. You are even willing to risk a lot for a little of the pleasures of life. Your love life is a heartwarming example of open sharing.

Sun in Sagittarius—Moon in Gemini

It's doubtful that you are still holding the same job that you held a few years ago. It's not that you can't keep a job. It's just that you have to move on before you suffocate in a stale situation. You could have been King of the Rails during the 1930s. When you wake up each day, you are tempted to start walking in the direction that your shoes happen to be pointed. If someone tries to influence your life, you feel that you are being threatened. You may react to that threat with an emotional outburst. But it's all show. Inside, you are cool. You are a great storyteller, and probably could make a living at it. That is, if you felt the need. As it is, you're happy just to get by. Your love life is a string of whistle-stops, where you pick up just enough to fill your needs.

Sun in Sagittarius—Moon in Cancer

You are one of our solid citizens. Confident, competent and cautious. You can make a success of anything you try your hand at. You are quick to learn and are interested in distant places and foreign cultures. Your intuition is dependable. You often use it to help you select meaningful friendships for yourself. You have a vivid imagination. However, it can sometimes backfire by presenting you with fears that live more in your mind than in your life. You have enough self-confidence to set yourself up in new surroundings under the most difficult circumstances. That's because you have learned how to tap your inner resources. You prefer a romantic love life. That will call for an affectionate and sympathetic partner, one who shares your need for a comfortable domestic life.

Sun in Sagittarius—Moon in Leo

You are probably very careful about picking out clothes for your wardrobe. They must be in good taste, yet cut out for tomorrow's look. They must give you the look of the leader. Everyone expects that of you. You expect it of yourself. However, your carefree enthusiasm must not be hidden beneath a cloak of dignity. You are aggressively interested in people and places. You approach both with the fascination of a child opening birthday presents. Your major problems are that you can become too prideful, and that you are already too careless in your judgments. That's because you believe everything that you see and hear. Your love life is intense, passionate and romantic. However, you need a partner who can remember to remind you how wonderful you are.

Sun in Sagittarius—Moon in Virgo

You probably had a newspaper route when you were a child. And you never missed a delivery. Once you make a commitment, you always meet your obligations to it. You have a keen awareness of what's going on around you. That's your sixth sense at work. And it works so well that you always feel sure of yourself when you have to opt for a risk. You have a charming way with words. Some would even say that you are eloquent. Call it what you will, you could sell ice cubes to the Eskimos and, with your restless spirit, you would like to try that. But you're not likely to leave the comfort of your conventional life-style. Your love life is also conventional. Your prudish outlook keeps the covers on any sensual displays.

Sun in Sagittarius—Moon in Libra

At a party you are the one in the middle of that circle of smiling faces and open mouths. You're usually holding forth on one of your imaginative schemes or utopian dreams. You handle that scene well. Unless someone asks for the blueprints. Your specialty is The Big Picture. Details are for the drones. You are dynamic in everything you do. And you want to be into everything. But somehow you never get around to it. Let's face it, you roll heavily toward laziness due to a lack of any compulsive drives or needs. You get on well with almost everyone. You can make compromises, but never with your principles. You are attractive to the opposite sex. That pleases you, since you like variety. But it would please you more if you could find that perfect mate.

Sun in Sagittarius—Moon in Scorpio

You come on pretty strong. Your ambition, determination and independence stand out like the muscles on a weight lifter. Especially when you think that someone is taking you too lightly. The intensity of your feelings outweighs your better judgment when it comes to supporting a rebellious fight. You are at your worst when you are trying to do your best. That's because your mind closes down to the ideas of others as you fall back on familiar biases and beliefs. Fortunately, you recover quickly from your defeats, especially when something exotic comes up over your horizon. You won't miss it, since you are always on the lookout. You are often torn between following your free spirit over the horizon or seeking salvation in more practical pursuits. Your romantic spirit is searching for its soul mate. But the rest of you isn't interested in waiting.

Sun in Sagittarius—Moon in Sagittarius

Someone else may see a dog chase a cat up a tree, and two birds fly out in a panic. But, for you, that would be the starting point for a new theory about the balance of the universe. The cat-dog relationship would be the conflict of life; the tree, an indifferent battleground; and the birds, the innocent victims of a Darwinian struggle. That's the way you see everything—in terms of their cosmic significance. With thoughts like that in your head all the time, no wonder you forget to pick up the milk on the way home. You have great difficulty with the practical details of daily life. Like paying bills. But somehow things always work out for you. You live under lucky stars. You turn every listener into a student. Your open mind never allows you to take a closed position on any issue. You are a romantic in your love life. You put your partner on a pedestal, while admiring his or her physical attributes.

Sun in Sagittarius—Moon in Capricorn

You find it easy to accept Darwin's view of the world as a dog-eat-dog jungle. All your perceptions tell you that he was right. That's why you feel so unsafe in your corner of the jungle. The way you handle this is to go laughing through life like someone whistling through a graveyard. Your clownish ways are your cover for your concerns. Fortunately, you are an ambitious person with a practical outlook. You work hard, are shrewd and have the imagination to overcome large-sized obstacles. But you drive yourself too hard, and don't spend enough time with others. Your sense of humor should make it easy for you to reach almost anyone. Since you feel so insecure, your love life is a search for someone with the sensitivity to see you and want you just as you are after you take off your clown costume.

Sun in Sagittarius—Moon in Aquarius

Even though you always know what you are doing now, you never know what you will be doing next. You are very colorful and usually can be found in the midst of your far-out friends. However, you are the one that stands out. You are the one that ferrets out the next adventure for others to follow in hot pursuit. You enjoy this game as long as you are in front of the pack. They accept your leadership because your enthusiasm is matched by practical common sense. Your problem is that you become stubborn and autocratic in dealing with the opinions of others. Fortunately, your charm gets you out of any tight spots. Your love life is an open experiment with unconventional and uninhibited sex. You need a partner who is as open as yourself, and equally firm in his or her need for experimentation.

Sun in Sagittarius—Moon in Pisces

Success may be just over the next hilltop. But you're not sure it's worth the effort to make the grade. You would rather settle into your snug valley and turn it into a garden of your own. You could sit there, giving yourself over to the whispering muses who call you to join them in gathering flowers or reciting poems. Or, better yet, writing poems. You need someone to admire. Someone to use as a model for your own development. Since you absorb the attributes of those who are around you, you should choose your friends for the attributes that you admire. The real world is not half as fascinating for you as the worlds you find between the covers of books. Your love life must be like a romantic novel. You are not interested in getting between the covers with someone who is insensitive to your delicate needs.

Sun in Capricorn—Moon in Aries

If someone tells you to do something, they better tell it right the first time. By the time they get back with different instructions, you have already finished the job. Your hardest job is sitting still, doing nothing. You get so involved in what you are doing that you lose patience with fellow workers who engage you in conversation. It's easy to see why they think you are aloof. From your point of view, they are lazy. One of the reasons you're so busy all the time is that you need an outlet for all that frustration and anger generated in your soap-opera home life. You look for the admiration and rewards from your job that others find from their family and friends. Your love life is unromantic, but passionate and experimental. You are looking for an uncompetitive mate.

Sun in Capricorn—Moon in Taurus

You are the one that most people would like to see as the head of their organization. You are hard on work and soft on people. You have the vision to set realistic goals, and the patience and determination to see them through. Your eloquence and gifts of persuasion are enhanced by your obvious honesty and concern for others and their needs. Your problem is that you are a little old-fashioned. You can't accept the rapidly changing lifestyles. That's what triggers all those angry outbursts and bouts of depression. Perhaps if you learned to express your feelings about them to someone you trust, they wouldn't back up as feelings of such frustration. Your love life needs a supportive partner who shares your needs for the good things in life.

Sun in Capricorn—Moon in Gemini

You're probably still looking for that million-dollar idea that will set you up for life. It's not that you don't have a million ideas already. That's your problem. You are interested in so many things, you can't decide where to place your bet. You could be a winner if you narrowed your choices down to a favorite. You would then have to overcome only one more hurdle—your impatience. You are so anxious to move ahead that you would find someone to do the work while you moved into long-range planning. But dealing with people, especially their emotions, confuses you. Perhaps you already sense that problem. Until you can think of a solution, you will probably submerge yourself under the protective workload of your present job. Your love life thrives on physical sex. Second to that, you enjoy a platonic relationship best.

Sun in Capricorn—Moon in Cancer

You never had it easy when you were growing up. So you learned how to look tough, and to act tough. But you haven't yet overcome all those fears and feelings of inadequacy. Your need for self-reliance doesn't allow you to accept your own emotional sensitivities. They are not the weaknesses that you think they are. They can put you in touch with others and allow their affections to reach you. You are basically a warm and compassionate person. You just don't let it come out. You have an eye for detail and a fantastic memory. With those you could crack into any profession. But if you go that route, you will be happier where you can practice as a loner. Your fears and insecurities have built walls separating you from those who really care for you. Your love life is a search for someone who can love you. But you have to love yourself before anyone else will.

Sun in Capricorn—Moon in Leo

You stand tall so that you can see over the heads of everyone around you. Anyone who crosses you will remember your revenge for years. Crossing you can mean anything from a minor insult to your pride to a major threat to your superiority. Your drive for power is so intense that you seldom notice that you are sacrificing your childhood principles along the way. But, you never forget a friend. You reward loyalty, well and often. But your pride and stubbornness keep you from making what could otherwise be easy compromises. Still, people like you, and the way you get things done. Your approaches are original and you work with a flair. Your love life is fun-filled and sensual. You are generous, but difficult to satisfy.

Sun in Capricorn–Moon in Virgo

If you had been working on the space program we would have gotten to the moon sooner. It is an understatement to say that you love to work. But you probably would not have been in the space program anyway. To you that would have been an idle fantasy. You're not one to waste your time foolishly. Your cold logic and matching ambition can be satisfied only by the responsibilities of a demanding career. You work well with people in spite of your apparent detachment. That's because beneath your hard shell you are sensitive to the feelings of others. Unfortunately, you expect so much of yourself that you can never be satisfied. Then you brood over the faults that you find with yourself. Your partner in love would like it better if you stopped talking about your work and got down to business.

Sun in Capricorn–Moon in Libra

People are always disappointing you. That's because you are looking to others for something that you can find only in yourself. No one can give you happiness or peace of mind. That comes from accepting yourself for what you are, instead of trying to be someone more acceptable to others. People will accept you once you learn to accept yourself. The sky won't fall if you assert yourself once in awhile. Your creative drives are blocked by your inner conflict between self-assertion and submission to others. Take a stand on a few issues, then notice that you have survived intact. That will put you on your way to further growth. Your love life is cushioned on a bed of romantic ideals. You need spiritual as well as physical supports to make you whole.

Sun in Capricorn—Moon in Scorpio

You were the playground terror. Tearing swings out of the hands of playmates, or shoveling sand into their hair. You were born bold and aggressive. It took ten years off your mother's life to tame you into a more submissive style. You can still be outspoken and sometimes cruel in your dealings with others. Not because you are insensitive to their feelings—when you hurt someone, you know what you are doing. You are keenly aware of what's going on around you, and you have strong opinions about everything. You express those opinions in a way designed to fetch an argument. You never avoid an argument unless you have to. Your emotional outbursts add color and flame to the fireworks. Your love life is rich in variety. Which, in your case, means that it is poor in fidelity.

Sun in Capricorn—Moon in Sagittarius

Somehow you have managed to confine your need for excitement and adventure within the constraints of a conventional career. You set high goals for yourself and easily achieve them. Your professional ambitions do not keep you from having a good time. You just bring your excitement into the job. Although you take things seriously, you are warm and outgoing with people. They enjoy your sense of humor and the way you can get off a profound comment with an offhand remark. You have a logical mind and an uncanny talent for seeing into tomorrow's needs by looking at today's trends. Traditions are important to you. Your moods range widely from the intensely serious to the wildly impulsive. Your love life is based on loyalty and dependability. You can be an ardent lover when it occurs to you.

Sun in Capricorn—Moon in Capricorn

When you search your mind for the pleasant memories of your childhood, you are stumped. You can remember responsibilities and chores. But not much fun. Perhaps that's why you have become so serious about life. Your survival depended on taking everything seriously. You always lived by the rules. You still need rules to live by. You need bureaucratic guidelines and corporate manuals to help you get through the day. Your climb to success is a matter of following them, one chapter at a time. You are tenacious enough and patient enough to take that route up the ladder. Your real problem is that you have lost touch with your own feelings and the feelings of others. It's never too late to reestablish contact. Your love life is driven by sex, put under cool covers.

Sun in Capricorn—Moon in Aquarius

You are caught between your respect for the past and your impatience with the future. You are fascinated by the changes and discoveries announced every week. And you want to blaze a few trails of your own. You are very perceptive and have the intelligence and drive to follow up on what you see as meaningful goals. But you're a loner, and your goals require an involvement with other people. You are the victim of your own deep feelings of insecurity. You stand a good chance of ridding yourself of those feelings once you allow yourself to become involved with people. Look for others who will give you the emotional support and encouragement that you need. Your love life runs on your charming personality. Yet your partners will find it hard to turn on your "intimacy" switch.

Sun in Capricorn—Moon in Pisces

You derive your pleasures from the persistent pursuit of a difficult career. You have the courage and strength to make your dreams come true. Creative imagination is your strong suit. Your handicap is your fear of being hurt. Your successes are slow in coming because you carefully pick your path so as not to hurt anyone. Guilt and confusion rush in when you imagine that you have done some wrong. You even feel guilty about being ambitious. Since you pick up on the emotions of those around you, you should associate with cheerful people with positive outlooks. Your sensitivity to the ills of the world keeps you facing the dark side of life. You must look the other way to avoid bouts of depression. Your love life is frustrated by your insecurity and shyness. A sensitive and caring partner is the simple cure.

Sun in Aquarius—Moon in Aries

It must be a frustration for you to have to stop so often to let others catch up with you. Your imagination and intelligence let you see and understand what's coming up before others are even aware of change. Impatient with efforts to communicate with people, you resort to giving them orders. Cooperation is difficult for you. That's because you consider people to be either confused or ignorant when they don't understand you. You are apt to respond to the shortcomings of others with emotional outbursts. But getting tough isn't the way to deal with people these days. You will just have to learn to be more open to the ideas of others. Your love life shows the mark of this same impatience. Your idea of being warm is to indulge in an occasional act of generosity.

Sun in Aquarius—Moon in Taurus

You are a born leader. And a good one. Except that your need for faithful followers is almost compulsive—not that you wouldn't lead them to a grand goal. That's the problem. Your goals are so grand that they would probably be beyond the realm of realism. Yet, you maintain faith in your goals and work diligently toward their attainment. You are as careful in executing your plans as you are in making them. You refuse to compromise with your principles. You are willing to take a risk, provided that it is not on Friday the thirteenth or that a black cat has not just crossed your path. You would be more effective if you were less stubborn. It's commendable to have a "stick-to-it" approach. But there are times when it's smarter to know when to "just-drop-it." Your love is imaginative, yet dependable and loyal. You seek a long-term relationship. That will require a patient partner.

Sun in Aquarius—Moon in Gemini

You can probably tell an interesting story about almost any place that someone happens to mention in passing. You are a natural explorer. You can't learn enough about foreign places and people. The future fascinates you, and you want to do what you can to make it happen sooner. Especially if you can bring in some of your own ideas of needed reforms. This preoccupation with the future can sometimes cause you to lose touch with the needs of the "now." Part of those needs should include your establishment of emotional ties with other people. That's not easy for you, since you prefer the role of the loner. Your love life shows those signs of the loner. You might connect with more partners if it wasn't for your detachment that blocks any efforts at permanent alliances.

Sun in Aquarius—Moon in Cancer

People would never accuse you of putting on airs. You are as comfortable eating at a hot dog stand as you would be at an expensive restaurant. You are very sensitive and sympathetic to the feelings of others. And your acts of kindness and compassion are not acts at all. You mean them. People feel comfortable with you because they trust you. Your mind is always searching for something new. Your curiosity is boundless. You also try to keep yourself actively involved with people, because you find that people help you overcome your fears and feelings of insecurity. Your charming ways assure you of their emotional support. Your problem is that if someone happens to hurt you, it hurts for a long, long time. Your love life is romantic and passionate. But you need mental as well as physical stimulation.

Sun in Aquarius—Moon in Leo

One side of you wants to treat everyone as an equal. The other side wants to be in charge of everyone. But you want to be the kind of boss that everyone loves. You stay up nights wondering how to strike that happy balance between being a nice guy and being in charge. Fortunate-

211

ly, you have learned some ways for obtaining the power and status you need while still treating people with thoughtfulness and compassion. Your authority is cloaked with appropriate dignity and charm. You are very intelligent and have great drive. But you have trouble making decisions. You don't know when to trust your head and when to trust your heart. Trusting your intuitions, you take impulsive actions which often lead to disaster. But recovery is quick. Success comes to you as a reward for the intensity of your commitment. Your love life is a search for the stability of a family life. Your partner finds it easy to put up with your moodiness as the price for your devotion.

Sun in Aquarius—Moon in Virgo

Some of your friends may think of you as a flesh-covered, unfeeling robot. They get that impression from your detached manner. Yet it's just that detachment that gives you the objective perceptions you need to assume control over the situations around you. Emotional involvements confuse you. It's not that you have no feelings. In fact, you have deep feelings. But they are reserved for the mass of humanity rather than the particular person. Your problem is that your detachment can cause you to slip into snobbery. Your keen eye is quick to spot the faults of others. But that doesn't mean that it's your duty to call it to their attention. Let up on them. And let up a little on yourself too. Your love life is an exercise in loyalty and devotion. That's because it's hard for you to get intimate with others.

Sun in Aquarius—Moon in Libra

It must amuse your friends to hear about your latest disappointment at the betrayal of a trust you placed in another person. Yet, you continue to have faith in the basic goodness of people. You are cheerfully optimistic, and you treat everyone with kindness and respect because of the need to be surrounded by many friends. Most of them return your kindness and respect. Since your own feelings take on the coloring of those around you, it is

212

important that you pick your friends for their positive outlook. Although friends are important, be sure to take some time out to be alone, just to keep in touch with your own feelings. Your love life is a search for someone who would look great on a pedestal. With your romantic outlook, that could be anyone. But beware that your pedestal partner doesn't step down on your tender feelings.

Sun in Aquarius—Moon in Scorpio

When you go to a party, everyone knows you are there. They fall into two groups: One group thinks that you are just great; the other thinks you should be thrown out. No one is neutral. You have a mind of your own. And you make that perfectly clear to anyone who tries to tell you what to do. Especially if it gets in the way of what you want. Mostly, you want the rewards of recognition and status that go with a position of power. You can be ruthless with anyone who stands in your way. You might save yourself unnecessary grief if you learned to bend with the wind instead of fighting it. You should try to channel some of your energies into those humanitarian goals that often cross your mind. Your love life is a series of on-again, off-again affairs. You are intense in your passions, which often lie expectantly at the other end of a short fuse.

Sun in Aquarius—Moon in Sagittarius

A smorgasbord is your example of the best way to live. You can pick and choose from among all the exotic and interesting offerings of life, ignoring the bland and conventional. That's your solution to the endless bouts with boredom. You are frequently inspired by your intuitional insights. But you seldom follow them up to a practical consequence. Instead, you are soon off chasing still other dreams or fantasies. Although you have intellectual abilities, you run from the classroom of books into the outdoor school of experiences, especially if you can find those experiences in distant places. Your need for independence borders on open rebellion. That will often give you the appearance of an eccentric. Your love life

213

is a continuous search for yet more novelty. You need a partner who is as unconventional as you are.

Sun in Aquarius—Moon in Capricorn

If you ever joined a debating society, you would be the darling of the team. You could easily win an argument in which you had to defend the virtues of rugged individualism. Yours is a blend of imagination and practical ambition. You can set yourself meaningful goals and then logically lay out a clear path for reaching them. Your decisions are free of bias or emotional confusion. You put on a charming front for your many friends, yet you manage to maintain a touch of detached independence. They don't realize that you expect others to be as self-sufficient as you are. Learn to be tolerant of those with less ability. That could help you to enrich your relations with them. Your love partner can depend on your loyalty, but you tend to overlook the romantic aspects of your relationships.

Sun in Aquarius—Moon in Aquarius

You may not qualify as an absent-minded professor, but you sure act like one. Your mind is always off on some fascinating mystery to be resolved. With your wide range of interests, that mystery can be the riddle of the Sphinx, or the secret of desalting the seawater. Your mind seems to have a link to the future. It's the kind of mind that finds tomorrow's solutions to today's problems. But before you find them, you will have to become single-minded enough to focus on one problem at a time. Your friends are attracted to you by your charm and your far-out ideas. However, some of them think that you are a little too far-out. Your love life is rich with partners who are attracted to your uniqueness. You share yourself freely with many friends, but always short of a romantic relationship.

Sun in Aquarius—Moon in Pisces

You have that faraway look about you that makes people wonder if you are all there. You seem to be in

214

several worlds at the same time. And yet you enjoy being with people, and they seem to enjoy being with you. You still believe that everyone is basically good and that they follow the same code of ethics that you follow. It is surprising that, with your openness to so many people, you haven't been thoroughly exploited. Perhaps there is some protective occult shield that guards you from the wolves of the world. You have creative abilities that could be used to express your vivid imagination. But you may need the help of friends to keep you at the discipline required to develop those abilities and to use them. Your love life is imaginative, and rich in its sharing of sensitivities. Which is why you need a partner of your own sensitivity.

Sun in Pisces—Moon in Aries

You may seem to be a shy, innocent babe in the woods. But you can take care of yourself in any situation. You are shrewd and cunning when it comes to taking care of your own needs. That doesn't mean that you aren't nice to people. But your needs will come first. Especially when they have to do with your security and the comforts of life. With your instincts you usually get what you want. You enjoy taking risks in your gamble for personal gain. But you are sometimes torn between your feelings of aggression and feelings of compassion for others. You resolve the resulting guilt feelings by acts of generosity. Guard against turning those generous impulses into ego trips for yourself. Also, guard against those temper tantrums. Your love life is focused on the imaginative aspects of sexual experiences. You demand too much from your partner, and you become upset when those demands are not met.

Sun in Pisces—Moon in Taurus

Somehow you have learned how to be helpful and generous without becoming a soft touch. That's because you place as much value on your own needs as you do on the needs of others. Therefore, you can easily say no when you feel that someone has made an unreasonable demand of you. And your no doesn't immediately trigger

215

a set of guilt feelings. You are a sentimental person who has to guard against overreacting to emotional situations. Take plenty of tissues to a sad movie. You also have a deep feeling for things of the past. You can become stubborn when you have to give up old things. Especially your old views and old opinions. You must learn to change with the times. Try to get your feelings out into the open. Your love life is a combination of sentimentality and generosity. You are a loyal partner who can be very affectionate.

Sun in Pisces—Moon in Gemini

You are probably an actor on the stage. Or in jail. You can play any role you want. Or pull off any con act in the business. Your intelligence, intuition and ingenuity can take you as far as you want to go in any direction. There's the rub—you have no direction. You must be on the move all the time. That means that you are more likely to be into schemes than into purposeful pursuits. You get by on your intuition rather than by thinking things out. You are easily influenced by the company you keep. Unfortunately, you seem to attract the fast talkers and seedy characters in life. If you ever found the right partner, one who had the patience to help you implement some of your better ideas, you would be an unbeatable team. Your love life is characterized by those lines, "When I'm not near the one I love, I love the one I'm near." You may settle down in later life.

Sun in Pisces—Moon in Cancer

You feel so good about yourself that you seldom feel the need for self-improvement. It's not that you have to correct any faults or flaws of character. You are very well-adjusted. But you have many latent talents that may never see the light of day. If you made the effort to develop them, they could add extra dimensions to your life. Whenever you try to do this, you usually quit at the first demands of the required discipline. Your best bet would be to get involved with people who are very active

216

in your areas of interest. Their enthusiasm can carry you along as you work on your own talents. You should try to get over that habit of feeling sorry for yourself. Your love life runs on your romantic feelings. You still have to work out those feelings of shyness that block your enjoyment of physical sex.

Sun in Pisces—Moon in Leo

You have a zest for living which you show to the world by your flamboyant dress and your colorful mannerisms. If only you had the self-confidence to go with that display of self-assurance! You give the impression of being able to accomplish great things. But as you approach a decision point that would launch you into a higher position, you find some reason to be excused. Your fears and insecurities restrict you to safer territories where your abilities cannot be challenged. Try taking some small risks now and then until you can build up more confidence in yourself. Also, start allowing yourself to be open to the ideas of other people. Your love life is based on your strict standards of loyalty. With the right partner, you are a tender and uninhibited lover.

Sun in Pisces—Moon in Virgo

You are one of those people who seems to have been born "old." As a child you were already conscientiously carrying out the responsibilities of obligations with a dedication that is the definition of the work ethic. You are somewhat shy with people. You approach everything with a cautious shrewdness. You can size up people quickly. And your intuitions about the situations around you are usually accurate. Your problem is that you are quick to find fault with yourself. It may be something you feel you failed to do. Or something that you think you should have done better. These become fester points for growing feelings of guilt. You then have to work harder to atone for those guilt feelings. It would be better if you spent more time with other people. Especially people who have a cheerful and self-confident outlook on life. You will soon find that you are feeling better about yourself too. Your love life is rich with devotion and affection. Your partner can keep it that way by giving you frequent reassurances.

Sun in Pisces—Moon in Libra

Few people can understand how you can become so ecstatic about a quiet walk in the woods. They cannot imagine the attunement you attain with the sounds of the wind, or the birds in the trees. Your problem is that you would rather stay in the woods than come out to face the harsh reality of life. Your way of coping with reality is to give in to the wishes of others, just to avoid the hassles. You feel that there is something wrong with standing up for yourself. It comes down to the fact that you don't want to hurt anyone's feelings since you can feel their feelings as though they were your own. Your need for security can lead you to seek an early marriage, or a less demanding career. Your love life is joyous. You are lost in love without losing control over your love situations.

Sun in Pisces—Moon in Scorpio

There's always something serious going on between your ears. Your keen perceptions bring in a steady stream of observations. These then become food for introspection that goes on at the most profound levels. With your mind, you can find profound meaning in cooking a pot roast. Your emotional sensitivities are equally active in responding to everything that goes on around you. That's why your surroundings are such an important influence on your life. You should make every effort to keep them as congenial as possible. You are reluctant to make changes in your life. You are even stubborn about changing your mind. You find it very hard to give up an opinion, or a bias, that you have held for a long time. Your love life is intense and sensitive. You want to keep your secrets, but you must know all those of your partner.

Sun in Pisces—Moon in Sagittarius

You're the one who goes out to look for the pony when you find the pile of horse manure on your front lawn. Your friends find themselves refreshed when they come in contact with your optimism. You need freedom from conventional constraints so that you can exercise your creative impulses. Those impulses are usually directed toward the attainment of intellectual goals. However, you tend to follow too many paths, without following up on one before starting up on another. You might be able to reach your goal if you made the effort to bring more discipline into your life. You often ignore the practical problems of life, convincing yourself that things are not as bad as they seem. You then expect that some stroke of good luck will come to your rescue. Fortunately, Lady Luck usually arrives just in the nick of time. You need full-time companionship in your love life. That means that you want a partner to whom you can be loyal, forever after.

Sun in Pisces—Moon in Capricorn

If someone brought you a pony for your birthday, you would complain about the piles of manure that would have to be picked up each day. Yes, you're a pessimist. You are keenly aware of everything going on around you. But you always seem to be more aware of the unpleasant things first. You even think of yourself in terms of your shortcomings rather than your virtues. You do have virtues, you know! Then, you try to make up for your shortcomings by putting every effort into building up a career. That career must be a one-person operation so that its success can be traced back to your efforts alone. Your perseverance will usually bring you that success you seek, part of which can be traced to your ability to organize everything into efficient, well-defined activities. You relate well to others, and they generally like to be with you. You hold back your affection in fear of rejection. Your love life depends on finding your security in the love of your partner.

219

Sun in Pisces—Moon in Aquarius

Your friends often wonder if you are paying attention to them as they are talking to you. No wonder. Your mind is usually a million miles away, chasing some thought back to its source. Still, there is another part of you in the room paying attention to every detail. You can be back in a moment, all ready to provide a most interesting answer to any question. Your interests tend toward the global issues centered on the problems of humanity. This focus on overall social needs makes you lose sight of the needs of specific individuals. You like people and they like you. But your moods are unpredictable, and may sometimes be upsetting to others. Try to be more open with your feelings. Your love life is based on the needs of friendship rather than the demands of physical sex. Your need is for an intelligent partner.

Sun in Pisces—Moon in Pisces

People often wonder how such an innocent, trusting soul such as you can make it safely through this hostile world. Yet you never worry about a thing. Your intuition never lets you down. It tells you what's going on around you—who is friend, and who is foe. Since you are not playing for the stakes of this world, you are seldom a threat to those who are in the rat race. Your charm is all you seem to require to meet your simple needs. Those needs are to express your creative urges that will require that you muster the necessary discipline to develop your latent talents. You will need the help of a sympathetic partner to keep you at those disciplines. Your love life is sensual, but not necessarily sexual. Your love is experienced more at the soul level than at the physical level.

There you have it. The way astrologers see the significance of your sun sign and moon sign. These particular interpretations are based on the perceptions of Jefferson Andersen (see references). Astrologers may differ from one another in matters of emphasis, but they generally agree on the major traits to be assigned to each sign. Also, astrologers would include the positions of other celestial objects in their analysis of cosmic influences on your life.

9
Making Use of What You Have Learned

Introduction

We have covered many things. You saw that the moon was always suspected of playing an important role in our lives. You followed the moon's motions around the earth and saw how those motions change the forces and fields which are the major influences in your environment. That environment affects your behavior by the way it changes your body chemistry. We then saw how the moon's influence on people can differ, depending on where the moon is with respect to the person's natal moon.

You know how to find the moon's phase and moon sign for any date and how to plot these in search of patterns between your natal moon and the moon at times of stressful circumstances. You have learned how to plot the natal conditions between you and someone else, to explore the likelihood of compatibility.

You learned how to use the Daily Moon Chart to find the time of day when the moon's influence is strongest or weakest. And to use the Moon Node Table to follow the moon's changing influences over the decades. These, along with the Moon Phase Table and the Decan Moon Sign Table are your tools for learning how the moon affects you. Let me review how these tools are used and suggest some ways to use them.

Checking the Past

Perhaps the easiest way to begin looking for moon influences is to look back at some of the more important events in your life. Many people still keep diaries. You don't have to have one of those detailed diaries that become treasure houses of poetically described experiences which become the golden memories of life. A simple business diary, or jottings on the pages of a calendar is all you need. In fact, it is easier to go through an appointment diary to find the dates of accidents, illnesses, vacations, sexual encounters, etc. Those are the kinds of dates you want to check on anyway. While you are going through your records, see if you can find the birthdates of friends and relatives, and some important dates in their lives.

Once you have collected your list of dates you can begin. It will save you a lot of time if you list your dates on a sheet of paper divided into columns as follows:

Date of Interest	Moon Phase Table ROW	Moon Phase Age in DAYS	Sun Sign DECAN	Moon Sign DECAN
June 15, 1979	I	21	9	35

I have shown how an entry would look in your listing. If you prefer, you can add two more columns to show the sign of the zodiac corresponding with the decan numbers. Listing your dates this way lets you use one table at a time for all dates of interest. You would find all row letters first, then move to Part II of the Moon Phase Table to find all the moon ages at the same time, and so on through the Decan Moon Sign Table.

Once you have the list of dates along with their corresponding phases and signs, you can begin examining them for patterns. First you would plot the event conditions against the natal conditions on the Moon Phase and Moon Sign plots to look for patterns of hard angles as de-

222

scribed in Chapter 5. You can make a supply of those charts by copying the blank form on the next page. But there are other things to look for as well. You recall that the environment changes from waxing to waning conditions at the four corners of both plots. You may find a crowding of events into those corners, which would indicate that your body is reacting to the environmental changes that occur at those corners.

In addition to the corners, you may want to keep your eye out for things that happen in the signs of the Ascending Node (and the hard angles to those signs). You remember that the Ascending Node is where the moon's orbit passes up through the ecliptic plane and is then in the same plane with the sun. There would be a special influence when the moon sign and sun sign happen to be in the sign of the Ascending Node. You can find those nodes from the Moon Node Table (Table 6) for the year of the event, or for your natal year. These nodes, and the signs at hard angles to them, have a way of showing up on difficult days.

Finding Your Ascendant

Those of you who are exploring astrology know that another important celestial reference point is your Ascendant, or "rising sign." That is the sign of the zodiac that was just coming up over the eastern horizon at the moment you were born. Whenever the moon passes through your rising sign it can have a special effect on you. You can use the Daily Moon Chart (Fig. 4–2) to find your Ascendant if you know the time of your birth. Here's all you have to do.

First, find your natal moon phase and moon sign. Then use the Daily Moon Chart to find the time of moonrise on the day you were born. Be sure to use the correction for moon signs (Table 5), to get the closest you can to the moonrise time that day. The moon sign tells you the sign of the zodiac that was just coming up over the horizon on the day you were born. That would be the Ascendant for a person who was born at moonrise that day. Someone born, say, two hours earlier than moonrise, would have an Ascendant that is one sign earlier along the

223

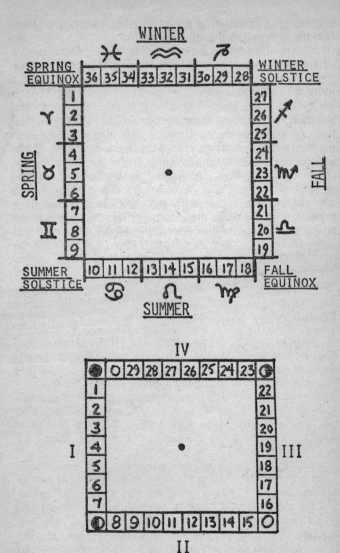

Fig. 9–1 Blank Moon Phase and Moon Sign Plots

224

zodiac. That's because it takes the earth two hours to rotate through one sign of the zodiac.

To find your Ascendant, or rising sign, find out how many hours there were between your birth time and the time of moonrise on the day you were born. For each two hours earlier than moonrise, move back one sign through the zodiac from the moon sign that day. For each two hours of a birth after a moonrise, move one sign ahead through the zodiac from the moon sign on that day. Moving back means to go, say, from Aries back through Pisces, to Aquarius, to Capricorn, etc. Moving ahead means to go from, say, Aries through Taurus, Gemini, Cancer, and so on.

Once you have found your Ascendant, you can place it on the Moon Sign Plots as a reference point to see how the event moon signs relate to it on special days.

Checking Partners

When you have the birthdates of other people, you can check for mutual compatibility by using the Moon Phase and Moon Sign plots as described in Chapter 6. You can use the plots to check out the patterns on special occasions, such as blow-ups or sexual encounters. You may find it interesting to keep track of the days during which sexual overtones are up front. If a woman, do they peak halfway through your menstrual cycle?

You can also check on the dates of increased male aggressiveness. We seem to know very little about cycles in sexuality in men. However, one woman alerted me to such cycles from her own experiences. She found that her men would make more calls and become more aggressive during Full Moons. I couldn't confirm or deny her findings. But I don't doubt it. You can confirm this for yourself, if only you keep score.

In addition to the examination of patterns on special days, you can use the plots to check on the hard angles between the natal conditions of two people. Remember, those hard natal angles mean that the event moon makes hard angles with the natal moons of both partners at the same time, causing stresses in both at the same time. That places a strain on a relationship. When you plot the natal

225

conditions of two people, you should place their Ascendants and the Ascending Nodes on the charts as reference points, so that you can check for hard angles between them. The patterns between these celestial indicators will be different between you and your friends from the patterns you find between you and those you try to avoid.

Checking on Births

You might also find it interesting to explore the claims of "astrological birth control." Those claims are that a woman is more likely to conceive, and to give birth, during the same phase of the moon that she was born under. You can check that easily enough by seeing whether your natal moon phase is the same as your mother's natal moon phase. And, if you are a mother, you can see if your children were born under the same moon phase that you were born under. Of course, if you are one of those women with irregular menstrual cycles, the bets are off.

You can also check on other claims that the sex of a child can be determined by the moon sign at the time of conception. You will need to find the date of conception first. You can use Table 8, Number of Days Between Any Two Dates, which follows. First look up the number that corresponds with the month and day of birth. Use the right half of the table to find that number. Then, subtract 266 days from that birthdate number and jot down the difference. Those 266 days represent the time from conception to birth. Now, look for the month and day that corresponds with the number you jotted down. That will be the month and day of conception. If the difference falls into the left half of the table, you will have to subtract one year from the birthdate year to get the year of conception.

Using the month, day and year of conception, find the moon phase and moon sign for that date. You should find that the moon phase at conception was the same as the natal moon phase. And the moon sign will be male or female, depending on the sex of the person whose birthdate you used. Male moon signs are Aries, Gemini, Leo, Libra, Sagittarius and Aquarius. Female moon signs are

226

NUMBER OF DAYS BETWEEN ANY TWO DATES

Days 1 – 365

Day Mo.	Jan.	Feb.	Mar.	April	May	June	July	Aug.	Sept.	Oct.	Nov.	Dec.
1	1	32	60	91	121	152	182	213	244	274	305	335
2	2	33	61	92	122	153	183	214	245	275	306	336
3	3	34	62	93	123	154	184	215	246	276	307	337
4	4	35	63	94	124	155	185	216	247	277	308	338
5	5	36	64	95	125	156	186	217	248	278	309	339
6	6	37	65	96	126	157	187	218	249	279	310	340
7	7	38	66	97	127	158	188	219	250	280	311	341
8	8	39	67	98	128	159	189	220	251	281	312	342
9	9	40	68	99	129	160	190	221	252	282	313	343
10	10	41	69	100	130	161	191	222	253	283	314	344
11	11	42	70	101	131	162	192	223	254	284	315	345
12	12	43	71	102	132	163	193	224	255	285	316	346
13	13	44	72	103	133	164	194	225	256	286	317	347
14	14	45	73	104	134	165	195	226	257	287	318	348
15	15	46	74	105	135	166	196	227	258	288	319	349
16	16	47	75	106	136	167	197	228	259	289	320	350
17	17	48	76	107	137	168	198	229	260	290	321	351
18	18	49	77	108	138	169	199	230	261	291	322	352
19	19	50	78	109	139	170	200	231	262	292	323	353
20	20	51	79	110	140	171	201	232	263	293	324	354
21	21	52	80	111	141	172	202	233	264	294	325	355
22	22	53	81	112	142	173	203	234	265	295	326	356
23	23	54	82	113	143	174	204	235	266	296	327	357
24	24	55	83	114	144	175	205	236	267	297	328	358
25	25	56	84	115	145	176	206	237	268	298	329	359
26	26	57	85	116	146	177	207	238	269	299	330	360
27	27	58	86	117	147	178	208	239	270	300	331	361
28	28	59	87	118	148	179	209	240	271	301	332	362
29	29	...	88	119	149	180	210	241	272	302	333	363
30	30	...	89	120	150	181	211	242	273	303	334	364
31	31	...	90	...	151	...	212	243	...	304	...	365

Days 366 – 730

Day Mo.	Jan.	Feb.	Mar.	April	May	June	July	Aug.	Sept.	Oct.	Nov.	Dec.
1	366	397	425	456	486	517	547	578	609	639	670	700
2	367	398	426	457	487	518	548	579	610	640	671	701
3	368	399	427	458	488	519	549	580	611	641	672	702
4	369	400	428	459	489	520	550	581	612	642	673	703
5	370	401	429	460	490	521	551	582	613	643	674	704
6	371	402	430	461	491	522	552	583	614	644	675	705
7	372	403	431	462	492	523	553	584	615	645	676	706
8	373	404	432	463	493	524	554	585	616	646	677	707
9	374	405	433	464	494	525	555	586	617	647	678	708
10	375	406	434	465	495	526	556	587	618	648	679	709
11	376	407	435	466	496	527	557	588	619	649	680	710
12	377	408	436	467	497	528	558	589	620	650	681	711
13	378	409	437	468	498	529	559	590	621	651	682	712
14	379	410	438	469	499	530	560	591	622	652	683	713
15	380	411	439	470	500	531	561	592	623	653	684	714
16	381	412	440	471	501	532	562	593	624	654	685	715
17	382	413	441	472	502	533	563	594	625	655	686	716
18	383	414	442	473	503	534	564	595	626	656	687	717
19	384	415	443	474	504	535	565	596	627	657	688	718
20	385	416	444	475	505	536	566	597	628	658	689	719
21	386	417	445	476	506	537	567	598	629	659	690	720
22	387	418	446	477	507	538	568	599	630	660	691	721
23	388	419	447	478	508	539	569	600	631	661	692	722
24	389	420	448	479	509	540	570	601	632	662	693	723
25	390	421	449	480	510	541	571	602	633	663	694	724
26	391	422	450	481	511	542	572	603	634	664	695	725
27	392	423	451	482	512	543	573	604	635	665	696	726
28	393	424	452	483	513	544	574	605	636	666	697	727
29	394	...	453	484	514	545	575	606	637	667	698	728
30	395	...	454	485	515	546	576	607	638	668	699	729
31	396	...	455	...	516	...	577	608	...	669	...	730

Table 8   Number of Days Between Any Two Dates

227

Taurus, Cancer, Virgo, Scorpio, Capricorn and Pisces. Remember, these are the moon signs at the time of conception, not the natal moon signs at the time of birth.

I am almost certain that you are going to be amazed at what you find when you check a few cases for yourself!

Setting Up Your Moon Calendar

Once you have caught up with the past, your attention will turn to the present and the future. You will find that as something happens, you will ask, "I wonder where the moon is today?" But you probably will be too lazy to get out the tables to look it up. You can overcome that problem if you make up a moon calendar for the month, using a calendar that gives you room to write something at each date. It's not that hard to do, and the once-a-month effort will be worth it.

Here's all you have to do. First, find the day of the New Moon in an upcoming month. If it isn't already marked on your calendar, you can usually find the dates of the major moon phases in the daily newspaper. Or, use the Moon Phase Table (Table 3) from Chapter 4. Once you have the date of the New Moon, you can number each calendar day with its corresponding moon age number, starting with the New Moon as day 0.

After you have the days numbered by moon age, circle the moon age corresponding with your natal moon phase. Then, count off 7 days to each side of your natal phase and place a square around those dates. These are the dates during which the moon will be square to your natal moon. These are the dates on which you should exercise a little more care, stay more alert than usual. And do the same on the date that is 14 or 15 days from your natal moon. Remember, that is when the moon is in opposition to your natal moon. You can note that on your calendar by a heavy underlining of that date. That's the date that most people were reported to have had their accidents, according to the "inconclusive" Sandia report.

After you have marked your calendar with the moon ages, you can then mark it to show the moon signs. You can use the Zodiac Moon Sign Chart for that (Fig. 4–1). Here's how.

First, notice which of the decan rows cover the dates of your month of interest. Then draw vertical lines between the dates on your calendar which would separate the month into those decans. Now, beginning with the first day on your calendar, notice the moon age that you wrote on that date. Use that moon age to find the moon sign on the decan row corresponding with that first day of your calendar. Place that moon sign in the space for the first day of the month.

Now continue across that decan row, copying out the moon signs corresponding with the moon ages for each of the days on the calendar. Continue this until you come to a vertical decan-separating line. That line tells you that it is time to drop to the next lower decan row to find the moon signs on that next segment of your calendar. The procedure is straightforward. You look at the moon age of a calendar date, and then find the moon sign for that date from the appropriate decan row of the Zodiac Moon Sign Chart. The vertical lines on your calendar tell you when to drop down to the next decan row to continue your readout of moon signs.

You will notice that the Zodiac Moon Sign Chart helps you to see when the moon passes through a cusp between two signs. You can show that by a slash line through that day on the calendar, with the appropriate sign on each side of that slash.

This may sound difficult as you read it. But when you follow these steps, one at a time, with a calendar and the Zodiac Moon Sign Chart in front of you, you will find that it is really quite simple. And fun. Try it and see for yourself.

After you place the moon signs on your calendar, be sure to circle your natal moon sign. Then count off 7 days from either side of the middle day of your natal sign, and mark those dates with a square around the moon signs there. These are the days when the moon is in a sign that is square to your natal moon sign. Actually, they are 6.83 days away, but 7 is close enough, and easier to plot.

229

After you do that, underline the moon sign that is 14 days away from your natal moon sign. That is the day that the moon will be in a sign that is in opposition to your natal moon sign. The dates of these hard angles—the squares and oppositions—are the dates you should be alert to difficulties.

You may also place other reference points on your calendar to help spot significant relations between the moon's position and events in your life. For example, you can show your rising sign, or Ascendant, on the calendar date for that sign. And, you can show when the moon will pass through the Ascending Node by using a symbol at that sign of the zodiac on your calendar.

As events come up during the month you should note them to see if there is a pattern with respect to these signs. You should remember that there are special conditions that arise at four specific signs. The moon crosses the equator at Aries and Libra, and it is furthest from the equator at Cancer and Capricorn. If you find that events cluster at any of these signs, it signifies some response to the changes in the moon seasons. If there are clusters of events at the Ascending Node (or at hard angles to it), that signifies there is a response to the moon's position with respect to the sun in the ecliptic plane.

Regardless of which pattern reveals itself first, you will soon become aware of it. That will be your first step in recognizing the influence of the moon's changing positions in affecting your life. From there, it is a matter of learning to anticipate those influences, and learning to cope with the stressful conditions they sometimes bring with them. It is also a matter of learning to recognize and ride the rising tides of energies which flow from the same sources to enrich our lives.

Finding Daily Patterns

It takes 24 hours from the time you see the sun directly overhead to the next time you see it directly overhead. That is the solar day. It takes 24.8 hours from the time you see the moon overhead until it is directly overhead again. That is the lunar day. The extra 50 minutes are needed for the rotating earth to catch up with the moon, which is revolving around the earth in the same direction.

There is clear evidence that many of our responses are still timed to a lunar day. For example, consider this excerpt from the magazine *Science*. "A psychologically normal blind man, living and working in a normal society, suffered from a severe cyclic sleep-awake disorder. Investigators showed that he had circadian [that is, daily] rhythms of body temperature, alertness, performance . . ." that were different from the 24-hour schedule. His "rhythms all had periods which were longer than 24 hours *and indistinguishable from the period of the lunar day.*" (Emphasis mine.)

It is also interesting that "there was a remarkable coincidence between his sleep onset and a local low tide." This problem of daytime sleepiness was found to be more common than suspected, and "not necessarily restricted to the blind." That may provide a clue to some of your own cycles of daytime sleepiness, or to other behavior which may be following a lunar day instead of the solar day. Let me show you how you can check that for yourself.

Suppose that you find yourself getting sleepy during times when there is no reason for you to be getting sleepy. Or, you notice that you are making an unusual number of errors, for no apparent reason. There are times that you can't keep your mind on a discussion during a conference, or you find yourself reading the same paragraph over and over again. Then there are the mornings that you spring out of bed, already wide awake, while other days you can't drag yourself out of bed after hours and hours of sleep!

The next time something like that happens, write down the date and the time. When you have a collection of such dates you will be ready to consult the Daily Moon Chart (Fig. 4-2) in Chapter 4. You will have to have a working copy of that chart. You can copy it on a machine or trace it off onto something that you can write on. Or, you can simply work on a piece of tracing paper taped to the chart in the book. Once you have a chart to work on, you can begin plotting the timing pattern of your experiences.

First, you will have to find the moon phase for the event date. Then, on the vertical line that represents that moon phase (in days of moon age), place a dot at the horizontal line that corresponds with the time of day that the experience occurred. Remember that Standard Time is shown on the left, while Daylight Saving Time is shown on the right of the chart.

When you have plotted your points you should find a pattern of dots which show when those experiences occur with respect to the passages of the moon from moonrise to moon noon, to moonset and finally to moon midnight. As you search for the pattern you should remember that there are two times each day when the moon exerts a maximum pull and two times that its pull is at a minimum. The minimums occur at moonrise and moonset. The maximum pulls occur at moon noon and moon midnight. If your points cluster around these pairs of lines, you can assume that the effect has to do with the gravitational forces.

However, suppose that the cluster of points has to do with the moonrise line, with few if any clustered near the moonset line. Then the moon's effect is not due to its gravitational forces, but rather its light, or electromagnetic, energies which arrive differently at moonrise than they would at moonset.

In using the Daily Moon Chart you should make the corrections for the moon signs when they are near Cancer and Capricorn. No corrections are needed if the moon signs are near Aries and Libra. Also, remember that the peak of the combined pull of the sun and moon occurs before moon noon when the moon phase is in the first quadrants (moon ages 1 to 7). The peak of the combined pull occurs after moon noon (and moon midnight) when the moon phase is in the second and fourth quadrants (moon ages 8 to 14, and 23 to 0).

Obviously, the pattern of your responses to the lunar day will be easier to detect if you have a larger collection of dates to be plotted at one time. They should be events of a similar kind. However, some of these events may be subject to influences other than the moon. For example, if you can't get out of bed after a night on the town, it wouldn't be fair to blame that on the moon, would it?

It might be interesting to see whether there are times of the lunar day that are better or worse for you, depending on when it is with respect to your natal time of birth. Perhaps here too, there are squares and oppositions (6- and 12-hour differences) with respect to the daily cycle which once served to tell us when to go forth, and when to stay put.

The natal time of birth for those born under a Full Moon, in terms of the lunar day, would probably be between moon noon and moonset. That's because most people are born between solar midnight and solar dawn. If you check the Daily Moon Chart you will see that these solar hours correspond with the time between moon noon and moonset when the moon's age is 15 days (Full Moon). Incidentally, you can also see from the chart that a child born under a Full Moon would experience 24 hours of continuous light on its first day of birth—half sunlight and half moonlight.

Some Research Projects for Fun

One of the nice things about having the tables and charts in this book is that you will be able to try your own research projects. It's one thing to hear about how something is affected by the moon. It's another to be able to check it for yourself. If you haven't already thought of things to look into, let me give you some ideas. Even if these don't turn you on, they may make you think of something that does. You would be surprised at how many important discoveries have been made by amateurs like yourself, with simple tools and imagination.

Consider the question of the time of birth. And its relation to the time of death. When are most people born in terms of their moon phase and moon sign? Claims for a maximum birthrate at the Full Moon are supported in the literature. But what is the most frequent moon sign? Or, what is the most frequent combination of moon season and sun season? What is the most frequent moon sign at death? How is that fatal sign related to the natal sign? How would you go about exploring these questions?

Once you have the moon signs for the natal and fatal dates, you can plot them on a chart, one against the

233

other. Twelve rows against twelve columns, one for each sign of the zodiac. The rows can represent the natal signs and the columns can represent the fatal signs. For each person place a dot at the intersection of the row and column representing the natal and fatal signs, respectively. After the points are plotted, look for clusters around certain signs across the rows and down the columns. Do there seem to be more points near the solstice signs or the equinox signs? Do the points seem to lie along "drift lines" that slope up or down across the chart? Clusters of points along such drift lines show that some relation exists between the natal and fatal signs.

You can then plot natal phase against fatal phase in the same way. In this case you'll need thirty rows and thirty columns, one for each day of the moon's age. The combinations of things to do are limited only by your creativity. You can plot natal phases against natal signs, natal phases against fatal signs, etc. One combination will suddenly stand out by offering a sharply defined pattern which then will lead to your discovery.

You can move from the question of individual birth patterns to population birth patterns. Does the long-term cycle of the moon's tilt affect birthrates? You can collect birthrate statistics over several decades and plot these against a time axis of the years covered. Then you can plot, on that same axis, the tilt of the moon's orbit over those same years. You will find that information in the Moon Node Table (Table 6) in Chapter 4.

You may find it even more interesting if you separate your birthrate statistics according to latitude of the populations. Of course birthrates are affected by complex interactions of many factors. And many things are affected by latitude, especially the climate. But the question is whether these other effects are amplified or attenuated when the tilt of the moon's orbit carries the moon far from the equator, or keeps it circling nearby.

Then too, you might consider the question of the effect of the moon on accidents and illness. Almanacs list the dates of major catastrophes for train and plane crashes, shipwrecks, earthquakes, etc. What were the moon phases and signs on those dates? Do they cluster at the Full Moon? Or at some combination of moon phase

234

and moon sign? Do the dates have anything to do with the Ascending Node that year?

Libraries carry several sources for accident and illness rates over the years. You can plot these rates in the same way that I suggested for plotting population birthrates. When you can get such rates broken down by month, are there seasonal patterns which change over a 9-year (line of apsides, or apogee-perigee cycle) or 18.6-year Metonic cycle? As you become familiar with the tables and charts in this book you will think of other questions that you might consider.

Those of you who are interested in financial cycles may enjoy looking for relationships between the moon and the ups and downs of the market. I am told that you can expect a correlation, although I have never looked for it myself. Since the market reflects the outlook of people and swings from bullish to bearish, it may reflect the lunar influences on the environment which drives behavior to those outlooks. You should look for more than moon phase patterns in the highs and lows. Perhaps a combination of phase and sign will reveal that key insight. I'm sure that if you find it I won't hear from you. But I may read about you and your riches.

Some of you may be celebrity watchers. You may watch the entertainment world, the sports world, or the political world. You can find the birthdates of your favorite celebrities in your local library. Keep those dates in a file. Then, when you see a news item that tells you of a specific success or loss, accident, illness or death, you can run a quick check with the Moon Phase and Moon Sign plots to see how the moon may have been involved in their problem. Or their success. You can also compare the natal conditions of pairs of celebrities to estimate the likelihood of a compatible relationship, as described in Chapter 6.

The problem with checking on celebrities is that they usually run such a stressful life that they respond to a very complex set of influences, making it hard to identify any one as a significant influence.

As I described these few ways for you to do your own research with the tables, I hoped that other ideas

235

occurred to you. You will be surprised to find how easy it is to do a research project, once you get organized. You don't need large computers. Just some imagination and the desire to look into the mysteries of life.

Keep Me Posted

There are many unanswered questions about the influence of the moon. I have tried to provide you with the information and the tools to help you search out some of the answers for yourself. Naturally, I am interested in what you may find. I hope that you find enough to write your own book. I'd love to read it. Even if you don't write a book, I'd still love to hear what you find. If something that I told you doesn't work for you, I would like to know that too. You can reach me by writing to Mort Gale, P.O. Box 210, Riverton, NJ 08077. I will be happy to answer your letters if you send along a self-addressed, stamped envelope.

I hope that you enjoyed reading this book as much as I did writing it for you. I hope you have a better understanding of how "outside" forces become the "inside" forces that drive your behavior. Once you recognize that, it becomes easier to steer a saner course through life.

Good luck!

References

Those who are interested in learning more about the various topics covered in this book can begin by looking at some of the following references.

General References

Carson, Rachel L. *The Sea Around Us.* New York: Mentor, 1954.
Dewey, Edward R. *Cycles: The Mysterious Forces That Trigger Events.* New York: Manor, 1973.
Gribbin, J. R., Plagemann, S. H. *The Jupiter Effect.* New York: Vintage, 1976.
Huntington, E. *Mainsprings of Civilization.* New York: Mentor, 1945.
Lieber, Arnold L. *The Lunar Effect.* New York: Doubleday, 1978.
Luce, Gay G. *Body Time.* New York: Bantam, 1973.
Watson, Lyall. *Supernature.* New York: Bantam, 1974.

Chapter 1—Moon Beliefs
Abel, E. L. *Moon Madness.* Greenwich, Conn.: Fawcett, 1976.

Adderly, E. F., and Bowen, E. G. "Lunar Component in Precipitation Data." *Science* 137 (1962): 749–50.

Bradley, D. A., Woodbury, M. A., and Brier, G. W. "Lunar Synodical Period and Widespread Precipitation." *Science* 137 (1962): 748–49.

Fielden, J. M. *Nagel's Encyclopedia-Guide: The Moon, or Selenology in its Various Aspects.* Geneva: Nagel, 1970.

Harley T. *Moonlore.* Detroit: Singing Tree Press, 1969.

Thomas, R. B. *The Old Farmers Almanac.* Dublin, N. H.: Yankee, Inc., 1978.

Chapter 2—How the Moon Moves Around the Earth

Clancy, E. P. *The Tides.* New York: Doubleday, 1968.

Glasstone, S. *Sourcebook on the Space Sciences.* New York: Van Nostrand, 1965.

————. *The Science of Astronomy.* New York: Harper & Row, 1974.

Moore, Patrick. *New Guide to the Moon.* New York: Norton, 1977.

Panides, N. *Introductory Astronomy.* Mass.: Addison-Wesley, 1973.

Thurman, H. V. *Introductory Oceanography.* Columbus: Merrill, 1975.

Chapter 3—How the Moon Gets to You

Becker, R. O. "Electromagnetic Forces and Life Processes." *Technology Review* 75 (1972): 32–38.

Brown, Frank A., Jr. "Living Clocks." *Science* 130 (1959): 1535–44.

Brown, Frank A., Jr., and Park, Y. H. "A Persistent Monthly Variation in Responses of Planarians to Light, and Its Annual Variation." *International Journal of Chronobiology* 3 (1975) 57–62.

Burr, Harold Saxton. *Blueprint for Immortality—The Electric Patterns of Life.* London: Neville Spearman, 1972.

Eckert, H. G. "Lunarperiodic Variation of the Phase-Angle Difference in Nocturnal Animals Under Natural Zeitgeber Conditions Near the Equator." *International Journal of Chronobiology* 4 (1976): 125–138.

Gale, Mort. *Biorhythm Compatibility.* New York: Warner, 1978.

Gauquelin, Michel. *The Cosmic Clocks.* Chicago: Regnery, 1967.

Gauquelin, Michel. *The Scientific Basis of Astrology.* New York: Stein and Day, 1969.

Gould, J. L. *et al.* "Bees Have Magnetic Remanence." *Science* 201 (1978): 1026–8.

N.A.S.A. "Possible Relationships Between Solar Activity and Meteorological Phenomena." *N.A.S.A. SP–366*, 1975.

Palmer, Bruce. *Body Weather.* New York: Jove/Harcourt Brace Jovanovich, 1977.

Piccardi, G. *See* Gauquelin, M., 1967.

Soyka, Fred. *The Ion Effect.* New York: Bantam, 1976.

Stolov, Harold L. "Variations of Geomagnetic Activity With Lunar Phase." *Journal of Geophysical Research* 69 (1964): 4975–81.

Chapter 4—Where Is the Moon Today?

Michelsen, Neil F. *The American Ephemeris.* New York: Astro Computing Services, 1977.

MacCraig, Hugh. *The Ephemeris of the Moon, 1800 to 2000.* Richmond: Macoy Publishing, 1951.

Chapter 5—The Moon and Bad Times

Lieber, A. L. "Homicides and the Lunar Cycle: Toward a Theory of Lunar Influence on Human Emotional Disturbance." *American Journal of Psychiatry* 129:1 (1972): 69–74.

"Solar Flares and Road Accidents." *New Scientist,* April 25, 1968.

Chapter 6—The Moon and Compatibility

Heuts, B. A., and Kop, P.P.A.M. "Month of Birth and Partner Choice in Marriage." Volume Five Supplement to *International Journal of Biometeorology,* 1974.

Chapter 7—The Moon and Women

Lacey, Louise. *Lunaception.* New York: Warner, 1976.

Malek, J. *et al.* "Characteristics of the Daily Rhythm of Menstruation and Labor." *Annals New York Academy of Sciences* 98 (1962): 1042–55.

Marx, Jean L. "The Mating Game: What Happens When Sperm Meets Egg." *Science* 200 (1978): 1256–59.

Menaker, Walter, and Menaker, Abraham. "Lunar Periodicity in Human Reproduction: A Likely Unit of Biological Time." *American Journal Obstetrics and Gynecology,* 77 (1959), 905–14.

Menaker, Walter. "Lunar Periodicity With Reference To Live Births." *American Journal Obstetrics and Gynecology* 98 (1967): 1002–4.

Chapter 8—The Moon and Astrology
Andersen, Jefferson. *Sun Signs and Moon Signs–An Astrological Guide to Your Secret Self.* New York: Dell, 1978.
Busteed, M., Tiffany, R., and Wergin, D. *Phases of the Moon.* Berkeley: Shambhala, 1974.
Leek, Sybil. *Moon Signs.* New York: Berkley, 1977.
Orser, Mary, Brightfield, Rick and Glory. *Instant Astrology.* New York: Harper/Colophon, 1976.
Quigley, Joan. *Astrology for Adults.* New York: Warner, 1976.
Rudhyar, Dane. *The Lunation Cycle.* Berkeley: Shambhala, 1971.
Townley, J. *Astrological Cycles, and the Life Crisis Periods.* New York: Weiser, 1977.
West, J. A., and Toonder, J. G. *The Case for Astrology.* Baltimore: Penguin, 1973.

Chapter 9—Making Use of What You Have Learned
Dept. of Commerce. *Earthquake History of the United States.* Publication 41-1 NOAA, Boulder, Colorado, 1973.
Dewey, Edward R. *Cycles—Selected Writings.* Foundation for Study of Cycles, Pittsburgh, Pa., 1970.
Miles, L. E. M. *et al.* "Blind Man Living In Normal Society Has Circadian Rhythms of 24.8 Hours." *Science* 198 (1977): 421–23.
Nelson, John H. *Cosmic Patterns.* American Federation of Astrologers, 6 Library Court, SE, Washington D.C., 1974.
Wilson, Louise L. *Catalogue of Cycles Part I—Economics.* Foundation for Study of Cycles, Pittsburgh, Pa., 1964.